D0098327

THE HORSES OF PROUD SPIRIT

Melanie Sue Bowles

Gayle Hunt

Pineapple Press, Inc.
Sarasota, Florida

Text and photos copyright © 2003 by Melanie Sue Bowles

Inquiries should be addressed to:

Pineapple Press, Inc.
P.O. Box 3889
Sarasota, Florida 34230
www.pineapplepress.com

Library of Congress Cataloging in Publication Data

Bowles, Melanie Sue, 1957.–
    The horses of Proud Spirit / Melanie Sue Bowles.— 1st ed.
cm.
    ISBN 1-56164-285-1 (hardback : alk. paper)
    1. Horses—Florida. 2. Proud Spirit Sanctuary (Myakka City, Fla.) 3. Animal rescue—Florida—Myakka City. 4. Bowles, Melanie Sue, 1957– I. Title.

SF301 .B648 2003
636.1'0832—dc21
                                                            2003007749

First Edition
10 9 8 7 6 5 4 3

Design by Shé Heaton
Printed in the United States of America

For Dusty

James Bowles

Acknowledgments

I AM GRATEFUL TO MY PARENTS, Rex and Ginny Foster, for compelling me to make a difference. And to my brother, Mark Foster, thank you for teaching me about the glorious world of books and reading. To my niece, Sarah Ross, thank you for sharing your love of horses with me, and thank you for being my friend.

I would like to thank Dr. Mark Davis, DVM, for your compassion, for always being there, and for your irreplaceable knowledge, despite which you are never afraid to admit you need to look something up. But mostly, I would like to thank you for always understanding the true purpose of this sanctuary.

Gayle Hunt: friend, artist, kindred spirit and fellow lover of horses. I have no doubts that without you this collection of stories would never have been started. And I know for a fact that without you they never would have been finished.

To David and June Cussen, thank you for your enthusiasm, your hard work, and for making the book a reality. To Alba Aragón, your intelligent input made it better. To Sarah Cussen, thank you for your enthusiasm. Your time and your hard work on this project mean the world to me.

An especially huge and loving thank you to my husband, Jim, for your calloused hands and your aching back as, uncomplaining, you once again clip your tool belt around your waist and tirelessly work to provide safety and shelter . . . a *home* . . . for "just one more" horse. Thank you for sharing your heart with me, and for letting me be who I am.

Contents

Introduction

MY FATHER WAS AN ADAMANT PROPONENT of John Donne's "No Man Is an Island" philosophy. And this is the way I was raised. My five siblings and I were shown by example and through lesson that we are not immune to our surroundings, and conversely, our surroundings are not immune to us. We were taught to respect the earth and her resources before environmental issues were a popular and daily topic on the news and in the paper. We were raised to be considerate of our neighbors and their property. And we were shown the rewards of being kind, honest, and trustworthy.

This is not to say we didn't make mistakes . . . in fact, just the opposite is true—we've all made some doozies. Maybe my siblings and I were not pushed so much to do great things, but we were given the powerful knowledge that it is profoundly rewarding and satisfying not to do bad things.

Once we all became adults with lives and families of our own, this concept has even become a rousing family joke at reunions and other gatherings. There is the inevitable discussion about the most recent divorce, or someone's ongoing financial fiascos. One of us shakes his or her head and says something like, "What a motley crew we are!" But someone else always loudly and enthusiastically reminds the fold, "Yeah! But we don't litter!" There is hearty laughter all around, yet deep down inside, each and every one of us is proud of this simple fact about who we are and where we came from.

One of the most life-altering lessons that I learned from both my mother and my father (I say "I" now, for even though we were raised by the same parents, I'm sure each of my five siblings came away with a different perspective on our upbringing) is that it's possible to attain higher levels of happiness, feelings of self-worth, and a genuine sense of accomplishment if we take the focus off ourselves—what we have, what we don't have, what we wish we had. We were encouraged to take a proactive approach to life and immerse ourselves in something we could be passionate about—be it woodworking, pottery, raising children, having a voracious appetite for books, whatever—rather than concentrating on ways to acquire more "stuff." And whatever we chose to be passionate about, we tried to remember that in one form or another, we are either taking from or giving back to the world around us. No man is an island.

Perhaps when we consciously try to conduct our lives in the spirit of giving back to the world, the gift of happiness, a feeling of self-worth, and a sense of accomplishment are simply there. . . . We do not have to seek them. It is this outlook on life, coupled with a culmination of events and experiences, that eventually propelled me toward my work with horses.

The stories you are about to read are true; the situations and events actually happened. However, the names of everyone but family members have been changed, and some people are a combination of several people. Due to their abusive past, most of the horses' names have been changed as well, along with their markings and breed to ensure their anonymity. These stories are the result of an emotional journey, the depths of which I could not have envisioned when I brought home my first horse, Cody (or Cocoa as she is affectionately called).

In many ways, these stories really come from the hearts and souls of the horses themselves. I am merely their voice. For if the truth be told, I have only walked along a chosen path—a path that has led me to provide some otherwise unwanted horses the peace and dignity they deserve. I did not go searching for the horses I have encountered along my journey and brought into our family (even though you might point out that I did indeed find most of them, and you would be right in saying so). Yet I truly believe that through some implicit power of the richness all around us, the reality is that they have all found me.

Cody

"I'VE BEEN THINKING ABOUT GETTING A HORSE." I blurted this out to my husband, Jim, one night while I was making dinner. We had just bought a home on five acres, about three or four months before. We were surrounded by other homes on five- and ten-acre plots and it seemed as though everyone had at least one horse on their property. Every day as I drove by our neighbor's pastures I was more and more in awe of their horses and couldn't seem to get the idea of having one of my own out of my head.

"A what!" Jim responded as he looked up from the bills he was working on at the kitchen counter. I just smiled at him and turned back to my cooking.

"You don't know anything about horses," he said, looking back down at the envelope he was addressing. "A horse," he murmured aloud, but it was more to himself, as if he couldn't quite grasp the idea of actually owning one.

He looked up at me again. "What brought this on?" But before I could answer, in a sort of thinking-out-loud tone of voice, he said, "We'd have to do a bunch of fencing. And we don't have stalls. Do they even need stalls?" Once again, before I could answer, he asked a second time, "But what brought this on, anyway? You don't know anything about horses."

"I can learn!" I laughed at him. "And I'm not bringing one home tomorrow. We could start doing some fencing on the weekends, and I was talking to Ellen about helping her out with her four horses. That will give me some experience and I'll be able to learn a lot from her."

"You still haven't answered me. What brought this on?" he asked with a smile.

"I'm not sure, except I can't stop thinking about it."

Ellen and her husband lived in the same neighborhood, just about a mile away. They had a small but very neat and orderly home on fifteen acres with an enormous barn as the focal point of their property. Although they were quite a bit older than Jim and I—they appeared to be in their early sixties—Ellen and her husband had befriended us shortly after we moved into the neighborhood. We had enjoyed numerous dinners together at each other's homes over the last few months.

Ellen was a very physically fit and slim, petite woman who always wore black riding breeches with black shiny boots up to her knees. There was an unwavering, stoic and severe, no-nonsense air about her. Her long black hair, with just a few streaks of gray, was always in a neat braid hanging down her back, a small red satin bow tightly holding the ends together her only show of frivolity. And it seemed as though she was never without a riding crop in her hand, even when she wasn't riding. Her movements were quick and direct, always with brisk precision as she flitted busily from task to task.

This perpetual motion was in sharp contrast to her horses. She had four enormous Thoroughbreds of various ages. They were all young, all were geldings ("mares are too moody," she would say), and all were for sale or would be soon. These horses were massive, so massive that they made Ellen look even tinier. They seemed to almost lumber as they walked; yet at the same time they were incredibly graceful. They made no unnecessary movements, in contrast to Ellen and her quick darting about. Their shiny coats glistened and gleamed with radiant health as all four walked like royalty, slowly and confidently, single-file into the barn with pure, dignified grace. I remember loving the clinking sound that their sixteen shoes made on the spotless concrete as each horse entered his own immaculate stall.

Ellen had raised these horses from babies, and she was grooming them for the show circuit. She spent every waking hour riding them and tending to their needs. When she had them trained in the discipline of dressage to a point where they could go no further with the abilities Ellen possessed, she sold them to someone who was able to take them to the next level. She would then buy more babies and start over. Ellen had no desire herself to show—she just loved horses, loved dressage, and was happy when the horses she raised could move on and further their training.

Jim and I agreed that we had the finances to start doing some fencing and I was going to be spending time with Ellen at her barn, helping out as much as I could, getting an education about horses. Unfortunately, it turned out that while Ellen seemed to enjoy my company and encouraged me to come around, she was a rather hard person to get to know. When I would ask a horse-care question, her answers were more often than not just a "yes" or a "no," never followed by the reason, or even her own opinion about a certain way she liked to do things. And for some reason I never understood, she wouldn't allow me to touch the horses or really even get near them. I had no desire to ride Ellen's horses and wouldn't have dreamed of asking. I knew without a doubt I wouldn't be able to handle them. They were professional athletes, and I understood that. I just wanted to brush their coats, learn to pick up and clean their feet, put a halter on, and lead them out to the pasture—but my requests along this line were repeatedly turned down.

After several weeks of sweeping Ellen's barn and cleaning her stalls, I still really had no idea how to put a halter on because I wasn't allowed near the halters, let alone the horses. I quickly decided two things—I needed to find another source of education, and I wanted a horse more than anything I have ever wanted in my life.

In no time at all, Jim and I (mostly Jim) had the fencing complete. We had decided to fence only the back half of the property, thinking this would be plenty for one horse. There was an outbuilding on our property, used as a workshop by the previous owner. Jim said he would partition off a section toward the back and put in a stall. He also made plans to build a run-in shed out in the pasture so the horse could get out of the weather on its own in case we weren't home. Now we just needed a horse.

Several weeks went by with me poring over the "horses for sale" section in the classified ads of the paper. I looked over the message boards at the local feed stores as often as I could. I had mentioned to several neighbors and friends that I was in the market for a horse and had even gone to look at a few at their suggestion. But none of the horses I saw seemed to be right for me, although truthfully, I wasn't even sure what right for me would be. And the horses I did like were either out of my price range or beyond my experience.

Then one day while on my way home from work I saw a handwritten sign for a garage sale. Now, poking around a garage sale is one of my favorite things to do, and even though I had groceries in the car I decided to turn down the road where the arrow pointed. Another handwritten sign in front of a large home situated on about ten or fifteen acres indicated that this was the place.

When I pulled in I noticed some horses out in a pasture. They were beautiful, and I watched them grazing as I walked up the driveway to all the furniture, clothing, lawn equipment, and household items set about for the sale. A woman sitting in a lawn chair stood up, and in a very dramatic way she waved her arms about and with a warm smile said, "Hello and welcome! Everything is for sale, everything! Including the house. We're getting rid of everything. No offer refused."

I smiled back at her friendly greeting and looked out toward the pasture. "Even the horses?" I asked.

She quickly placed a hand over her heart and looked at me in mock horror. "Lord, no! Not the horses! I could never part with those horses; they are like my children! Except unlike my children they don't cause me any heartache or grief." She grinned at me and I laughed at her bubbly personality.

"Are you looking to buy a horse?" she asked.

I told her I was, but I needed to find an extremely calm one as this would be my first horse and I was very inexperienced. She held up her hand and without saying a word she walked into her house. In just a few minutes she came back outside holding a scrap of paper with a name and number written on it. "You call this woman and I'll bet she'll have a horse that's just right for you."

I never even looked around at the items she had for sale, I was so excited to get home and make the call. After my groceries were put away I dialed the number on the little scrap of paper. The phone rang, and rang some more. I was just about to hang up when a young child who seemed to be out of breath picked up. "H'lo!" she quickly said.

"Ah, hi. I was calling about a horse you have for sale. May I speak to . . . " I looked down at the paper in my hand to read the name.

"Which one?" the child asked impatiently.

"Which what?" I asked.

"Which horse!"

"Oh, well, um . . . I'm not sure. Someone gave me your number and . . . " That was all I managed to get out when suddenly the phone was set down with a loud thud and I heard the child yell, "Ma! There's somebody on the phone askin' 'bout a horse, but she don't know which one." I sat there squirming about the fact that I had exasperated this child and waited for her mother to pick up, presumably the person named on the piece of paper I held in my hand.

I could hear a booming voice in the background yelling instructions about scrubbing out some buckets and other such chores, and as the voice got closer and the phone was picked up the instructions continued to boom. I had to move the phone away from my ear until she finished shouting and was ready to talk to me. But when she hollered "This is Alma " into the phone, it was clear that the booming voice was the normal way she talked.

Alma Parker made her living from horses: buying, selling, trading, and giving lessons. She assured me there would be a horse at her place that would suit me. She had more than ten for sale. Alma gave me the directions to her ranch—she was about an hour's drive away—and I headed right out.

Turning down the overgrown narrow dirt road, I wasn't really sure I had followed the directions correctly. There were no street signs. Alma had only said it was the second dirt road to the right. This was the second dirt road to the right, but after I had gone about a half mile I stopped, not sure if I should proceed or back out down the road because there seemed to be no place to turn around. As I debated about what to do, two young girls on horseback suddenly emerged from a blind drive that I hadn't even seen for all the overgrown brush. I leaned out the window and told them that I was looking for Alma Parker's place. They tossed their heads back to the drive they had just walked out of and one of them said, "This is Miss Alma's."

I waited for them to pass, then turned into the driveway. Pulling into this drive was like pulling into another world. I'm not sure what I expected, but it certainly wasn't the complete and total bedlam I now faced. Everywhere—literally everywhere—there were kids, dogs, chickens, potbellied pigs, goats, ducks, cats, kids and more kids, and horses, all loose and running everywhere! The pandemonium and cacophony were overwhelming!

"Oh my," I muttered to myself as I stuffed my keys into the pocket of my jeans and started across the dirt parking lot.

There were kids trying to scramble up on horseback all by themselves, other kids already on horseback recklessly riding wherever they pleased. A few kids were trying to help other kids up on horses, and some were trying to pull others off. Some were laughing, some were crying, some were fighting, and others were just minding their own business.

Dogs were barking at the kids making the most noise, pot-bellied pigs were squealing and running under, through, and around the horse's legs, goats were jumping on and off picnic tables bellowing out their opinions. I even saw a duck calmly sitting on the rump of a horse, his bright yellow feet standing out in sharp contrast to the horse's black coat. The chaos was only made worse by the fact that there didn't seem to be any adult supervision anywhere. It was completely beyond me that any parent would drop a child off into this confusion and simply drive away. I could barely absorb it all.

And amid all this insanity, there stood the horses: heads down, eyes unfocused, tails absently swishing at flies. Even in my gross inexperience I could tell that it wasn't because they were exceptionally well behaved that they put up with this craziness—they were simply numb.

And I could also see why Miss Alma's voice boomed—it had to. I heard her before I saw her back by a long row of shed stalls.

"You kids fill them water buckets, ya hear me? None of y'all are gonna ride till that's done!"

I started to walk back to where she was, careful to pick a route that would avoid the highest concentration of kids, animals, and puddles of muddy water. When I reached her she was busy clipping the long winter coat from a horse, but she continued to shout instructions to a group of older kids over the horse's back, the ones supposed to be filling water buckets, I assumed. Alma saw me walk up but didn't acknowledge me. She was dressed in men's jeans and wore a man's work shirt. The scuffed and dirty cowboy boots she was wearing looked to be men's also. Her large hands were strong and covered with tiny little cuts and scrapes in various stages of healing, and I could tell that the dirt stains in the lines and creases were permanent. No amount of scrubbing or soaking would ever remove the grime.

I stepped around the horse and into her line of vision. "Hi. I called a bit ago to look at some horses you have for sale," I said. She barely glanced at me but turned off the electric clippers she was using and stood up straight. She put her hand in the small of her back and grimaced while she stretched, then looked past me toward a horse tied to a hitching post in front of a small building.

"There," she said, nodding her head. "That'd be a good one for you." The whir of the clippers resumed and she went back to shaving the horse.

I turned and looked at the horse she indicated, then looked back at Alma, unsure about what I was supposed to do. Did she mean for me to wait while she finished up, or should I go over to the horse? I didn't know proper etiquette when looking at a horse for sale. She saw my hesitation. "Go on over and get you a saddle from the tack room there. Take her for a ride. You'll like her. I've already had my group of eight and nine year olds on her."

I walked over and stood beside the horse. I'd worry about telling Alma that I didn't have the first clue about how to saddle one later. Maybe she would just ignore me and I'd be able to skip right over that little embarrassing shortcoming in my knowledge of riding. Besides, I didn't even know if I would like the horse. If I didn't, I wouldn't have to worry about it. If I did and I wanted to ride, well, I'd just have to 'fess up. And looking back now, I shouldn't have liked the horse. But there was something indefinable working to bring this horse and me together that day, something bigger than my pathetic lack of knowledge about horses, and something bigger than the mare's pathetic looks.

They'd named her Duchess. They told me she had been at Alma's for less than a week. I could see that she was a bit thin and that her coat was rather dull, but I thought surely this would be easily taken care of. I'd just give her some good quality feed, bathe her, and brush her coat, and just like that I'd have a good riding horse.

What I didn't know in my painfully naïve ignorance was that she was full of parasites and that her teeth were so bad she could hardly eat. I didn't know that her severely overgrown and split feet were going to be a problem that would require shoeing her and months to heal.

And I also didn't know that she was so fed up with humans that when she had the energy to protest being handled, she would indeed protest with all her might, and she and I would embark on a journey of lessons and learning like no other I had ever experienced since or before. And make no mistake, I would be the student and she would be the teacher.

I was still standing beside Duchess when Alma came striding over, shouting instructions over her shoulder at yet another group of kids. "Well?" she hollered at me as she slapped Duchess on the rump. The mare barely lifted her head.

"She seems very sweet. I wouldn't mind riding her to see if I can handle her. I'm not real experienced."

"Oh, you can handle her. I've put small young'uns on her and let 'em go. Go on and saddle her." Alma waved her hand at the tack room she had mentioned earlier.

Crap! I thought. I am such an idiot! Why am I looking to buy a horse when I don't even know how to saddle one! Who does stuff like this? This is crazy! I should have taken more time to hang out with friends and other neighbors who have horses way before I ever even started to look for one. I felt like a complete fool.

"Um . . . I mean I'm *really* inexperienced. I, ah . . . I don't know how to saddle a horse. I mean I know which way it sits and all, but I don't know how to tie that little knot thing that goes around that strap," I stammered.

Alma's expression never changed as she looked me up and down, then slowly her eyes squinted into slits and she knitted her brows in such a way that said she was wondering what sort of freak of nature was standing before her. Without taking her piercing eyes from mine she screamed, "Betsy! Come saddle this horse for this lady!" And then for my benefit, because I was clearly too stupid to grasp the concept of what she had just yelled to Betsy, she added, "Betsy will come on over and saddle her." Unable to endure another second of Alma's steely glare, I looked down to the ground and mumbled a "thanks" to my shoes, which I noticed were inappropriate for riding, as Alma strode away.

Betsy couldn't have been more than nine or ten. And she had to be Alma's daughter because she strode just like her.

"You ride western, don'cha?" Betsy asked as she stomped up the wooden steps to the tack room, not bothering to hide her irritation over this interruption from whatever it was she had been doing. When I heard Betsy's voice I realized this was the child I had exasperated earlier on the phone.

"I, ah . . . I don't really ride, yet."

"Why ya buyin' a horse?" she hollered at me from the top step, her eyes squinted and her brows knitted together just like her mother's as she looked at me in total bewilderment.

"Western's fine, a western saddle will be fine . . . western," I nodded and continued to chastise myself for my foolishness that even a ten-year-old child could plainly see. I could feel beads of sweat running down my back and soaking my armpits. I looked at the palms of my hands and they were shiny with perspiration, all of which I blamed on the humidity of the day, not the fact that this woman and child had made me feel like the most useless person on earth. But something compelled me to stay on course. To this day I don't know why I didn't go running for my car and forget this entire insane idea of buying a horse. Or at least wait till I had more knowledge.

But Betsy had finished saddling Duchess and was handing me the reins before I even knew what happened. I took the reins from her and turned to watch her walk away.

"Where should I ride?" I called after her. Betsy stopped dead in her tracks. I saw her take a deep breath as she turned to face me, and very slowly, enunciating every word, she said, "On the horse path," as she pointed to a large hand-painted sign two feet to my right that said "Horse Path."

After a short but very quiet ride on Duchess, I felt certain that I wanted to bring her home. I can't put my finger on how or why I came to this decision, but I knew without a doubt that I wanted her. Alma came over as I stood at the same hitching post Duchess and I had started from just thirty minutes before.

"Well? She's real sweet, isn't she?"

"Yeah, I like her." I said. "What are you asking for her?"

For twelve hundred dollars Alma Parker hauled Duchess to my doorstep, handed me her lead rope, and was headed back to her own ranch without a backward glance. My neighbor Karen from down the road had seen the trailer pull in. Karen knew I had been searching for a horse, and after Alma had left, she walked over, anxious to see what had been delivered.

Karen stood looking at Duchess, the excited smile she'd had just moments before while walking up the drive draining from her face. Then she looked at me, and then back to Duchess once again. Karen tried to regain the excitement she'd had before she'd gotten a good look at my new horse.

"Oh! She's a Thoroughbred!" she said, her voice sort of trailing off.

"Is she?" I asked, excited that Duchess was a Thoroughbred only because Karen sounded excited that Duchess was a Thoroughbred. At least I think she sounded excited; maybe it was disbelief. I'm not sure now. Anyway, Karen quickly snapped her head around to look at me, apparently concerned that I didn't seem to know this little fact about the horse's breeding.

"Did you have a vet check her out, Mel?" she carefully asked.

"No," I answered.

"Did you have anyone go with you, someone who knows a little bit more about horses?"

"Um . . . no," I said, shaking my head.

"Did they give you any paperwork on her?" she asked with a furrowed brow.

"Nope." My shoulders were starting to sag.

"Do you know if she's been wormed?"

"Well, it wasn't mentioned," I responded.

"Her stomach seems a little bloated for as ribby as she is," Karen continued, relentlessly letting the wind out of my sails.

"You didn't ride her, did you?"

I perked up at this. "Yes! I rode her!" I happily answered in the affirmative, and proceeded to tell Karen that she behaved perfectly and I handled her just fine. But apparently this wasn't the answer Karen was looking for either.

"I don't doubt she was easy to handle. Her feet probably hurt so bad she can't do much arguing. See how long and split they are?" My shoulders sagged once again as I looked down to Duchess's feet where Karen was pointing.

"Do you know how old she is?" she asked.

"They told me she was nine," I said. Karen cupped Duchess's chin and looked in her mouth while telling me that you can sometimes tell a horse's age by looking at the teeth.

"Well, listen . . . " she said as she released Duchess's chin. "I need to get back home. Congratulations on your new horse!"

"Wait! How old do you think she is?" I asked, as Karen started to walk away.

She turned back to look at me, her face revealing the sympathy one feels for the very ignorant or the incurably insane.

"Oh, I'm not a vet. It's hard to say. But I do think you should get her looked at. I'll give you the number of the vet I use. And I don't think I'd ride her till her feet were looked at. She walks like she hurts." And she was gone.

I didn't bother to tell Karen that I couldn't ride her if I wanted to. I didn't have a saddle yet. And even if I did have one, I didn't know how to put the stupid thing on, I thought as I kicked the dirt.

The next morning, the depressing conversation with Karen gone from my mind, I grabbed Duchess's shiny new purple halter and raced out to bring her up to the lean-to Jim had recently built. I couldn't wait to brush her coat and comb her mane. I felt like a little kid. Duchess was happily grazing in the pasture we had created just for her and I went to her side. She stood patiently as I held the halter up, turning it this way and that as I tried to figure out how it went over her head.

Confident that I had it right, I turned to face my new horse and slid the halter on. There was a bounce to my step as I went forward, leading her up to be groomed. But suddenly I felt a tiny jerk, then heard the clang of the halter's buckles on the ground. Oops! I had forgotten to hook the throat latch and Duchess had put her head down, letting the halter slip right off her head. I got it right the second time and started off again. This time when I came to the end of the lead rope and felt that same little jerk, I was stopped dead in my tracks. I turned to look at Duchess and saw that she had her head high in the air, her face turned to the side, and she was rocked back on her heels, looking more like a stubborn mule than the elegant Thoroughbred that I had just recently been informed she was.

"Don't you want to be brushed?" I asked her. She indicated that she did not wish to be brushed by lifting her head even higher, removing any slack there may have been in the lead rope, and I didn't have a clue how to change her mind. Defeated in less than thirty seconds, I went to her side, slipped the halter off and went back in the house.

"I thought you were going to brush your horse," Jim said when I returned to the house so fast.

"Well, Karen said that I should have a vet look at her. I think I'll do that first." This was my lame answer for lack of anything better to say.

"Before you brush her?" he looked at me knowingly but graciously refrained from any additional comment. "Why does Karen think a vet needs to look at her? What's wrong with her?"

"Apparently numerous things, but she was vague," I told him defensively. He just nodded.

I made an appointment for Duchess to get a check up the following week. In the days waiting for the vet to come I became very good at putting her halter on and taking it back off, because that's all she would let me do. I also renamed her Cody.

When the vet arrived I met him in the driveway and we introduced ourselves. He asked if the horse was up and ready, and I told him I was having a little trouble getting her to cooperate.

"Let's see what we can do," he said, and took the halter from my hand. We walked out back and the doctor slipped the halter over Cody's head and started to bring her in. She did the same thing with him that she had been doing with me and adopted her stubborn mule position. But without missing a beat the doctor gently flipped the tail of the lead rope at her flank and she jauntily stepped forward to follow him. Oh.

From little ten-year-old Betsy incredulously asking me why I was buying a horse when I didn't know how to ride, and Alma's piercing stare when I revealed I didn't know how to saddle one, to Karen's list of questions, none bringing the response she sought, I had been humbled and reproached and was beyond embarrassment regarding my ignorance. I simply told the vet leading my horse that I was new to all this, as if it really needed explaining.

"Okay, what do we have here," he began as he pulled out a clipboard and started to write. "How old is the horse?"

"I'm not sure," I began. I started to explain what I was told by the person I bought her from and what Karen had said. He held up his hand and nodded, saying we'd figure it all out.

"When was the horse last vaccinated?" he asked.

"I don't know," I admitted.

"Did you get any paperwork of any kind?" I shook my head, starting to feel that same sinking feeling I felt the day Karen came over when Cody first arrived.

"Okay, a bay Thoroughbred . . ." He wrote this down and bent over to look back between her legs, apparently deciding not to trust me with this little query. "Mare . . ." he straightened and looked at her forehead, ". . . with a star," he concluded as he wrote down the rest of his findings. Then he turned to me and handed me his clipboard, trying to make me feel useful, I presumed, and he cupped her chin in his hand and lifted her upper lip. "She's just about fifteen years old," he said, releasing her chin.

After a lengthy examination, for which Cody stood like a perfect lady, the vet determined that she would need to be vaccinated, which he did right then. Then the incredibly long and sharp points on her teeth would need to be filed so she could eat properly, which he also did right then. Cody also had sores and ulcers in her mouth caused by her long teeth cutting into her cheeks, and the doctor wanted her on antibiotics for two weeks. She would need to be wormed, and he wrote down the products I should buy and instructed me how to administer them. And she would need to be seen by a farrier. He recommended putting shoes on all four feet and not riding her until the horrific splits and the severe thrush on her hooves had healed and grown completely out. And she needed to gain about two hundred pounds.

Then he asked me if someone had given Cody to me or if I had paid for her. "I bought her from a woman named Alma Parker," I told him. He looked at the ground as he pursed his lips and moaned, "Hmm . . ."

"Do you know her?" I asked.

"Well, she's got a reputation. I'm afraid she saw you coming."

"Ha!" I laughed ironically at the polite way he worded that. "I'm pretty sure I *announced* myself way before she saw me coming."

Jim was absolutely wonderful and I am grateful to this day that he never made one single comment, seriously or in jest, about my foolishness and the money some spouses might have said was wasted on a horse I couldn't ride. He never mentioned the hefty vet and farrier bills Cody generated in less than one week of ownership. For in the days and weeks that followed we both came to love her very much, and it was a pleasure to watch her out our living room window, contentedly grazing and getting healthier every day. I chose not to be mad at those who had so blatantly taken advantage of my ignorance and instead looked at this as a valuable lesson. The first of many to come.

The months went by and during this time, while Cody regained her health, I was able to work on my horse-handling skills. I had no problems leading Cody up to be groomed now. I knew how to pick up her feet, clean them, and apply the medication to combat the thrush. She was calm and gentle and usually stood with her head down while I fussed over her daily, and I always finished up with several apples and carrots for her as a treat. Everything was going beautifully. I also purchased a saddle.

Finally the day came when Cody's feet had completely healed

and the shoes could come off. She had gained a good amount of weight and looked slick and glossy. One day Karen happened to be over and pointed out the dark shiny dapples glowing through her coat and covering her rump. I had never noticed them before. Karen said I should be proud to have brought Cody so far—the dapples were a sign of good health.

I had spent the last six months or so taking Cody bags and bags of apples and carrots. She followed me around like a puppy dog; we were partners, and I loved her dearly. I could tell by the way she acted that she was going to tote me willingly around on trail rides as gentle as a lamb. My dream of going for long leisurely walks on horseback was just around the corner. And if someone had told me what was about to happen, I would have told them they were crazy and laughed in their face.

I was full of confident excitement and long-awaited anticipation of this first ride as I put my new saddle on Cody and fixed the new bridle in place. I led Cody around the barn and out to the driveway. I then double checked the saddle and the bridle, making sure everything was properly situated and buckled. Cody seemed to be a little nervous, but I thought maybe she was just excited about going on a trail ride. I patted her neck and then, grinning happily, I stepped up into the stirrup and swung my leg over her back.

I was feeling for the other stirrup when suddenly Cody's head shot high in the air. In an instant her eyes were rimmed in white, wide with some unseen fear, and she was twisting her head from side to side. I was startled by her behavior, but before I even knew what was happening, or how to respond, she started to jig sideways, prancing and stepping higher and higher as I struggled to stay on her back. I held the reins tightly, pulling back, trying to make her stop this prancing. Her head was turned sideways and she opened her mouth wide, trying to push at the bit with her tongue. The wild look on her face terrified me. She was snorting now, making a ragged, harsh noise through flared nostrils.

I had gained no control as Cody started backing up. Suddenly, she reared a few feet up off the ground and with both front feet still in the air she spun around and we were moving down the drive in a jerky rapid trot. In my frantic scrambling to stay on her back I had somehow dropped the reins. The dirt on the driveway was flying as she stepped sideways. Then, tripping over her own feet, she started moving backwards. Clouds of dust were billowing as high as her chest with every step. She started spinning in circles, each rotation taking us farther down the drive, her head still high in the air, and her eyes still wild and rimmed in white.

Suddenly, her back leg hit the wood fence that ran along the pasture. It startled her so that she lurched forward, almost unseating me. Desperately, I kept trying to grab the reins, to no avail. And each time I reached forward along her neck my arm came back slick with her sweat. I couldn't believe how fast she had become covered in sweat. Her neck and shoulders were soaked, when just moments before she was dry. My throat constricted with fear as I struggled to keep from falling. I had no idea at the time what I was doing to cause this terrifying ride, but getting off her was foremost in my mind. I just didn't know how to do it!

We were almost to the road now. We lived on a very quiet dead-end street, but all I could envision was her spinning wildly onto the pavement, me clinging to her mane and the saddle horn for my life, and both of us getting hit by a car. This was the motivation I needed to bail out, and I recklessly slid off her back, the momentum of her frantic prancing pitching me hard to the ground. The second I was off her back, Cody immediately stopped her wild display. She was breathing hard, and the veins in her neck showed through the dripping sweat like a road map, but she had calmed right down. Totally confused by her behavior, I sat there on my rump, looking up at her, trying to catch my breath as I wiped tears from my eyes. I'd never been so scared in my life.

Cody never left my side as I sat on the ground. She couldn't seem to stand still, and she was breathing very hard, but she stayed right beside me. After a few moments I stood to walk her back to the barn. We were standing at the hitching post and I was trying to take her saddle off. Cody suddenly pinned her ears and turned her head to me. Her teeth were viciously bared and she tried to bite me, which she had never done. Then, as I stood in front of her removing the bridle, Cody lifted her powerful leg to strike at me, her sharp hoof missing my upper thigh by inches. I couldn't get over what had just happened when I tried to ride her, and I couldn't believe that she was trying to hurt me now! For months this horse had been like a little kitten. I felt like I could do anything with her. And now, in less than a half-hour's time, I was terrified of her!

I put her halter on and started to lead her out to her pasture, but she began to prance and jig sideways, throwing her head and dancing all around me. "What is wrong with you, girl!" I pleaded with her to stop. Inside the gate of her pasture I reached up to undo her halter. I barely had it unlatched when Cody reeled away from me, almost knocking me down, and galloped off.

That evening I called an acquaintance of mine who had grown up with horses and told her what had happened, seeking some advice.

"Well, not knowing her history, it could be anything. You said she's a Thoroughbred and about fifteen years old? She could be off the track. It would have been years since she was raced if she's close to fifteen now, but maybe that's all she's ever known about being ridden. Or just the fact that she hasn't been ridden in years could cause her to react the way she did. The saddle may have been hurting her, or the bit. Or, it might have been you. Maybe she pranced just a little, but it was enough to scare you and you may have pulled back on her mouth and tightened your legs, making her prance more, trying to get away from all the pressure you didn't even realize you were putting on her. Maybe she's been really abused. It could be a combination of several things. There's just no telling." I asked my friend what she thought I should do. "Sell her. She's too much horse for you right now, and you're too inexperienced."

I felt completely deflated.

I decided to leave Cody alone for a few days and give us both some time to calm down. I took her grain out to her as usual and dropped some apples in her bucket, but that was about it. After some time had passed I grabbed her halter off the hook and went to bring her in to brush her just to see how she reacted to me. She let me slip the halter over her head, but as we got closer to the outbuilding where I kept her saddle she started to prance nervously, almost walking all over me as I kept moving to stay out of her way. At the hitching post I slipped the lead rope over the rail and tied a loose knot. All the while I was trying to soothe her, talking softly, petting her neck, but I kept my eye on her—she was acting like she was going to explode. Then suddenly she did just that.

Cody started to blow great bursts of air loudly through her nostrils while backing up till all the slack in the lead rope was gone. I tried to calm her as I stepped to the hitching post to untie the knot so she didn't get hurt, but I had tied it wrong and it tightened on itself. I couldn't undo the knot. When she came to the end of the rope she leaned back even further. Harder and harder she struggled against the constraints, almost down into a sitting position. All of a sudden the metal buckle on the halter snapped in two and Cody fell backwards, landing sideways on her haunch. Then, with hooves flashing, she scrambled to her feet and was gone like a bolt through the gate to her pasture.

We wondered briefly if maybe there was something by the outbuilding that was scaring her, but Cody behaved uncontrollably anywhere on the property almost the instant the halter was put on her head. The next few weeks were a nightmare. In addition to trying to bite me when I attempted to brush her, and dangerously striking out with her front leg whenever I stood at her head, she had now started running into me or pulling back to get away from me whenever I tried to lead her. I couldn't go five feet without her prancing and jigging and trying to run circles around me.

I had no idea how to handle any of this, but I needed help. It never entered my mind to take my friend's advice and sell Cody. I asked Jim if we could afford a professional trainer to come out to the house and work with both Cody and me.

The woman I hired came highly recommended. She was trained in dressage, was partial to Thoroughbreds, and went on and on about how beautiful Cody was the second she laid eyes on her out contentedly grazing in the pasture. However, after less than forty minutes of trying to work with us, the woman told me that my horse-handling skills were elementary at best, and I had no business owning a horse until I acquired more knowledge. But what was worse, she added that even then, this horse would need someone far more knowledgeable than I could ever hope to be and pointedly announced that I had no natural instincts or common sense about horses. "You need to get rid of this horse! She's going to kill you," she finally scolded. And she indicated that she did not wish to continue as our trainer.

Clearly, I was painfully ignorant about horses; I was not trying to delude anyone, including myself. But I did not agree with this woman that I had no affinity for them. I stood silently as the woman admonished me—and my dreams. But I was impotent in my defense because I had no words to describe what I felt in my heart for this horse. I simply stuck my tongue out at her as she drove out my drive.

Next, I sought the advice of a casual friend who had always owned horses and earned a living starting and training young ranch horses. I figured surely a tough old cowboy would be able to help me deal with everything Cody was doing. He lasted a few minutes longer than the dressage trainer, but his advice was pretty much the same, except not nearly as delicate. He told me that this was just the way Thoroughbreds are—they're hyper and excitable. They're good for nothing but running, he said. "No offense, Mel, but you need to put this horse out of everyone's misery, includin' her own, and put a gun to her head."

"Thanks, friend," I told him. "But no thanks."

Before, during, and after having these trainers come out, I started talking to anyone and everyone I could think of who knew anything about horses, seeking their knowledge. I received some decent advice, as well as some pretty shocking and abusive suggestions. But mostly, nearly all those whose advice I sought thought that I should sell Cody and look for a horse more suitably matched to my level of skill.

And again, this was not an option. I felt something deep in my soul for this horse, and I believed with all my heart that her problems stemmed from the fact that I didn't know how to communicate with her, coupled with the life she had led. She had been shuffled around from owner to owner, never forming a bond. I could see in her eyes a sensitivity and intelligence that had been stepped on and snuffed out, probably her entire life. For this inner light to glow with all the radiance I knew she possessed, she needed to trust. And I would do whatever was necessary to learn to communicate with her and show her that she could trust me.

How though? I lived in a neighborhood surrounded by horse people and horses. From all these people I had learned how to halter a horse, lead a horse, saddle a horse, groom, feed, and tend to a horse. But when I would ask these same people, "How do I communicate with my horse?," the answer from most—not all, but most—was always the same, and this answer, for me, was unacceptable. To this day I cringe with a sadness for all horses when I hear these words: "You need to get mean and show that horse who's boss. She's just trying to get away with all she can and take advantage of you." And I don't understand, nor will I ever, how this is communication.

I simply don't believe that horses are capable of scheming to "get away with all they can." To me this is anthropomorphism at its worst, and anyone who believes that an unwanted behavior displayed by our horses is based on the horse's ability to plot and devise ways to take advantage of us humans clearly has no understanding of what drives and motivates the species.

I refused to adopt this erroneous philosophy of showing the horse who is boss, even though it was told to me over and over again by numerous horse people. There must be respect, certainly, but more than anything there needs to be trust. And this respect and trust must be mutual. I was determined to learn to communicate with Cody in a language she understood, her language. Perhaps, it was time to go to the horses themselves.

I had always thought horses were beautiful to watch, but it had never occurred to me until just then to watch them to *learn*: to watch and observe how they communicated with each other. I became captivated observing the tiniest interactions between them, the slightest slant of their ears, which could mean anything from a dozing relaxation to an acute awareness of danger. Their eyes, their mouths, their tails, their legs, everything conveys some distinct form of communication.

Out for a walk one day I stopped to watch a neighbor's six horses in the pasture jockeying for position at the water trough. There was a woman outside and she saw me at her fence line and came over to say hello. We had never met before. She told me her name was Tommi, and after we had introduced ourselves, I commented that I was enjoying watching the interaction of her herd. She smiled at them, following my gaze, and said, "Yeah, they're funny, aren't they? That one horse who's making the others move out of his way is the guy who's always in charge."

I glanced over at Tommi with a look on my face akin to having a revelation. That one sentence, a casual response to my offhand comment, was the beginning of changing my life with Cody and bringing us full circle to a mutually profound, meaningful, and united relationship.

All the way home that singular thought kept drumming in my head: The one that makes the other one move is in charge; the one that makes the other one move is in charge. From the very beginning, practically since Cody and I had first been together, I had spent every moment with her getting out of her way. Trying to keep from getting stepped on or shoved and knocked down. She had been pushing me around like a dominant horse pushes around his subservient herd mates.

As soon as I got home I went directly out to Cody's pasture. She was grazing but looked up when she saw me and came right over. After sniffing me up and down she realized I had come empty-handed and went back to eating grass. And that's when it all hit me, like a slap in the face—I was nothing to her. I understood that horses have a "pecking order," but I never realized that Cody had pulled me into this herd of two—and she had promptly placed me at the very bottom. We weren't even partners or equals. I was nothing more to her than a carrot dispenser.

In my ignorance of equine communication I had allowed this to happen. I was the person who brought her grain, carrots, and apples, that was it. I was not a partner; she spent all her time trying to avoid being with me. I was not a source of security, foremost in the hierarchy of equine needs. Whatever had upset her that day we rode, it was clear to her that it had upset me even more. She had to have sensed my terror that day. And all her instincts told her she could rely on me for nothing in the form of protection or decision making. Nor was I a playmate. I offered her no challenges or stimulation. I offered her no physical comfort or mutual grooming, something so fundamental in the equine herd.

Amazingly, I was ecstatic at this discovery. If you don't know what the problem is, how can you fix it? But now I knew what the problem was. I was nothing to her. And now I could fix it.

Although not really sure how to fix it, I wanted to start immediately and decided to take my cue from Cody. She continued to wander off and graze, oblivious to my presence. I took up her rhythm, put my head down, relaxed my shoulders and meandered around the pasture with her. Almost like I was grazing too. I even went so far as to stomp the flies off my legs, like she was doing. For over a half hour I mimicked her moves and trailed along beside her, the whole time remembering that sentence my neighbor Tommi had just said to me. I recalled the more dominant horse in Tommi's pasture walking briskly toward the others at the trough, his shoulders square, his ears pinned back, and how he was sort of nodding his head at them as if to say, "Move along!" The moment the other horses moved out of his way, the dominant horse would relax his posture and everything remained peaceful. I tried it now with Cody.

In one movement, just like the dominant horse, I too squared my shoulders, my arms tight at my side, and walked at her steadily, nodding my head and thrusting my chin in her direction, my brow furrowed and my eyes glaring. Cody lifted her head to look at me. She wasn't alarmed, but she moved off and out of my way. I was astounded. For months this horse had been walking all over me, making *me* move. But now, she moved out of my way. And the second she did I stepped to the spot she had just been grazing, claiming it as my own, and relaxed my posture. I felt like I was going to cry. I had just communicated with Cody like another horse would communicate with her.

It was such a tiny bit of progress, but I knew it was the beginning. Within the next few days I went by Tommi's house again. I felt like I had learned more from her in a casual five-minute conversation than I had in months of talking to others. It turned out that Tommi was a wealth of information and readily shared all the knowledge she had.

She loaned me books and introduced me to the philosophies and techniques of world-class horse trainers who believe in equine communication in the truest sense—communication that allows the horse to be a partner and respond out of understanding and a desire to participate, rather than fear or pain.

I spent the next weeks and months pouring over the books Tommi loaned me, trying all the different techniques each trainer had developed. Tommi even came by many times to help out and work with Cody and me, showing me how to enhance the skills I was learning. I spent hours and hours out in the pasture with Cody, just watching her and trying different bits of equine body language, as best as I could in this human body. She always responded.

All of this input from Tommi taught me that I needed to continue to educate myself. She encouraged me to expose myself to as many different concepts and training methods as I could and then take bits and pieces from each one and apply what works for my personality, my horse's personality, and our special situation. She taught me to take from many trainers what I think works instead of just using all the ideas from one trainer.

The transformation in both Cody and me was remarkable. Cody had become calm, confident, friendly, respectful, and truly

happy. I too was calmer and more confident, and had a new respect for her as well. I was no longer terrified of her and understood more and more each day about how to develop a partnership between human and horse in place of the one-sided and dangerous relationship we had had for the last several months.

Cody seemed to glow in this new relationship we shared. She depended on me for more than just food, and she looked forward to the ground work we did almost daily. I also purchased a book on equine massage and relaxation stretches and began using the techniques on Cody. It was amazing to watch as she resisted at first, then let out a huge sigh and gave in freely to the movements. When we finished she would lay her forehead against my chest and let me hug her head. I would lay my cheek between her ears, the tears in my eyes speaking volumes of the love I felt for her. I could see the beginnings of a radiant light in her eyes, and I knew they soon would shine with a trust both for me and the life I had felt deep down in my heart that we could have together. This was a new beginning. ☕

Cody looking pretty for the camera.

Rex and Strut

WHEN YOU HEAR THE NAME REX IN A BOOK ABOUT HORSES, it may bring to mind a great big stocky draft horse. But Rex was my father, and he was neither big nor stocky. At just five feet six inches, he never weighed an ounce more than 140 pounds his entire adult life.

"Wha'cha doin'?" I called out to him as I got out of my car. He was standing on a ladder at the back of the used boat that he had just purchased a little more than a week before, busily wiping off the fiberglass transom with an old rag dabbed in mineral spirits. Jim and I were newly married and lived around the corner from my parents. I had stopped by on my way home from work, as I did practically every single day.

He straightened from his work and smiled at me. "I've settled on her name," he answered, patting the trailered boat sitting in their front yard. "I'm just getting ready to put these on." I saw the stack of peel-and-stick letters piled on the top platform of the ladder.

"Oooh! What's it gonna be?" I asked.

"You'll see," he chuckled.

This boat was a very sore subject with my mom. My parents had retired from Michigan to this Gulf Island home just a few years before. I was in my twenties at the time, working and on my own, but I was a bit of a mama's girl and had followed them to Florida.

Since the move, Dad had repeatedly expressed a desire to own a boat so he and Mom could take advantage of the abundant waterways Florida had to offer. Mom was adamantly against this idea. She felt they were too old and inexperienced to handle the larger boat the Gulf waters required for safety. The little freshwater lake we lived on in Michigan was no preparation for the difficult tides and sudden storms of the west coast of Florida. And every time he mentioned buying a boat she would firmly tell him, "Well, you'll be out there on the Gulf all alone, because I'm not going with you."

"Oh, Ginny," he would cajole, "you might go with me." He never believed for one minute that she wouldn't go with him—if he did indeed buy the boat—and neither did we.

She was absolutely stunned when he came home one afternoon after doing some errands with a used thirty-two-foot cabin cruiser of dubious seaworthiness in tow. He had not given her any indication that he had found a boat he wanted to purchase, and she was furious that he had not consulted her.

I stood watching him happily prepare the back of the boat to receive the letters. I took note of how many were in the rather tall stack and pondered what name he had come up with—although I was sure it would be named after Mom in some manner. In fact, since the beginning of their marriage almost fifty years before, every boat, car, or anything else that required christening was always given some form of her name, Virginia May. Even at the small lakefront parcel we owned back in Michigan, Dad had erected a sign proclaiming it "Virginia's Beach."

"Has Mom settled down about all this?" I asked.

"Oh, she will," he answered confidently as he picked up a V and peeled back the paper revealing the sticky backing.

I saw *Virginia May* take shape as he pressed the Y of her middle name in place. A considerable stack of letters still remained and I wondered what he was up to.

"What do you think?" he asked.

"Are you done?" I responded, my eyes shifting to the remaining letters.

He picked up an O, and with mischievous glee he chortled, "Oh, no! Wait'll ya see!" as he turned back to lettering the boat.

"Oh, Dad! Mom's gonna kill you!" I told him once all the letters were in place. I was laughing in spite of myself. This faded lime green boat, the one Mom declared she would never step foot on and Dad was sure she would, was officially named *Virginia May or She May Not.*

I believe that Rex was a genius. However, like most geniuses, he was labeled everything from an endearing character to an eccentric lunatic by those who failed to recognize his unique brilliance. My own opinion of him waxed and waned as I went from having a youthful exuberance for his antics, to being a rebellious teenager embarrassed to be living in the same house as this nutcase, to finally developing into a mature adult with an understanding and genuine appreciation of his talented intellect and soaring imagination.

The garage of our childhood home was a source of fascination to me. A car would not fit within its walls, but it was not what you would term cluttered. Rather, it was more like organized chaos. The walls were lined with rows and rows of shelves that held every conceivable type of container, from shoe boxes and cigar boxes, to Styrofoam egg cartons and cardboard food boxes, to those plastic trays that cookies come in to keep them from breaking. And stored inside this myriad of containers were all the normal things you might expect—nuts, bolts, washers, screws, and nails. There were also boxes of screwdrivers, files and rasps, hammers, clamps, paintbrushes, and pliers. And there were trays of glues and adhesives, paints and thinners, solvents, solutions, and sandpaper. But there were also things that most people would consider trash and would have thrown away.

Rex saved the caps, tops, and lids off everything. And he actually had three separate shoe boxes labeled in black magic marker: caps, tops, and lids. For apparently there was a difference. He saved blown tire tubes, useless umbrellas, busted rake handles, moldy foam rubber, broken aluminum lawn chairs, axles and wheels from old toys, cracked leather belts, broken glass. . . . This was only the tip of the iceberg, and everything hung from the rafters and burst from every corner.

Forming aisle ways were stacks and stacks of scrap lumber, half sheets of plywood, bins of old clothes that he used as rags, bins holding dowels of every circumference, and used two-by-fours of every length. There were towering piles of bricks and concrete blocks, rolls of tarpaper, rolls of plastic, rolls of screen. Shelves and benches were scattered with small engines, electric fans, blow dryers, and kitchen appliances—all in various stages of repair in Rex's ongoing quest to fix and improve everything mechanical.

Along with his own professional-quality drawings and diagrams, the walls of the garage were covered with foldout "how-to" schematics from *Popular Mechanics*, full-color maps from *National Geographic*, and faded black-and-white photographs of different completed projects from his youth, including a boat he built from scrap.

He was admired by some, despised by others—but whatever the neighbors thought of him they all came to him when they needed something fixed.

I was still young enough to be enthralled by his unconventional ways when I went to him to ask for a new set of handlebar grips for my pink banana-seat, stingray bike. In my haste, I had let it fall one too many times on the concrete and the plastic had scuffed away, exposing the metal. "Well, let's go see what we can put together," he responded as he wheeled my bike into the garage.

As a teenager, these very same words would make me cringe with embarrassment over the way he usually put something together. I remember asking my mother once why we couldn't just go to the store like the rest of the world and buy new when something broke. Why did things always have to be repaired from the junk out in the garage? I craved normalcy then and only wanted to fit in. But at age nine, I was still intrigued.

I stood beside him in the garage as he slowly pivoted in a circle, my bike leaning against a workbench. "Mmm hmm . . . that's what we need!" he exclaimed. I watched as he mounted a stepladder and crawled into the attic. "Here, take these," he said after a moment of shuffling a few things around. He was lying on his stomach across the open rafters, and I reached up to take the two umbrellas that he was passing down just as he cried, "Watch out, now!" He was a very strong man, very athletic. His small size made him quick and agile. I stepped back and watched with amusement as he rolled through the rafters, headfirst. He dangled there and easily did a few chin-ups, then dropped to the floor like a cat, a billow of sawdust puffing around his feet.

"What're we gonna do with these?" I queried, wondering how umbrellas would come into play in the replacement of my handlebar grips.

"Hang on, you'll see," he said as he walked over to the rows of shelving and peered into the boxes and containers there. Rifling through select ones, he finally found what he wanted, and I saw him toss whatever it was in the air and snatch it firm in his grasp as it fell. He found a second one and did the same thing, grinning happily and mumbling about how they'd "fill the bill." Next, he grabbed an old garden hose hanging from a nail on the wall and set it on the workbench.

The necessary parts were assembled; now we needed the tools. He placed a tube of silicone, a tube of some sort of glue, a utility knife, and a pair of scissors beside the garden hose.

He handed me the scissors and told me to cut four very thin strips from each of the colored sections of the umbrella fabric, about twelve inches long. Then I was to cut two strips from the white section the same length as the others. While I did this I watched as he pried the old grips off my bike and set them next to the hose. Then he used the utility knife to cut two pieces of the garden hose a similar length. He smeared silicone on the bare metal of the handlebars, then took the two pieces of hose and worked them into place. The two items that he had tossed into the air earlier turned out to be the bright yellow caps from some long-ago empty bottles. He made a small slit in each one, and once I had my ribbons cut, he folded them in half and inserted them into the openings. He ran glue all along the inside of the caps, securing the umbrella fabric in place, and then worked the caps onto the ends of the garden hose.

So there they were—the dull green of the old garden hose, the blue, green and white of the umbrella fabric streaming down, held in place by the cheery yellow caps, all blending gaily with the bright pink of the banana seat—my new grips. I proudly tooled off to join my friends, blissfully unaware for several more years that they regarded my dad as odd.

My very first vehicle was a 1968 Ford Econoline van. The engine ran like a top, but the interior and body needed tons of work. The summer of my eighteenth year, Dad and I set out to make it shine. We gutted the inside and sanded and reinforced the rust spots with fiberglass. Then we insulated and paneled the sidewalls and put plywood down on the floor and carpet over that. Dad found some old bus seats that were in great shape at a salvage yard and installed them in the back, along with the hinged storage boxes he had made from scraps of plywood stained and shellacked to a glossy finish. The interior complete, we were ready to begin on the outside, and we did the same to the rust spots there, sanding and patching the holes with fiberglass. Then we went off together to the auto body shop to pick out paint colors.

Dad had a tendency toward the gaudy and I begged him to let me choose the colors without his input. I picked out a pale green for the bottom panel and a soft yellow for the top portion of the van. Across the yellow, we planned to do some pin striping with the green to tie it all together.

I could tell he was disappointed by my choice. He liked to make a statement, let people know he was coming. After all, this was the man who painted our clapboard house sometime back in the fifties, alternating each board with hot pink and chartreuse green. We never understood his motivation for doing this, other than the fact that he thrived on being different. I'm only grateful that my mom and older siblings wailed with embarrassment loud enough that he finally returned it to a pleasant yellow before I was old enough to realize the hideousness of the situation.

I was thrilled with the results the day we painted my van. Dad was a pro with a compressor and spray gun. There wasn't a single run or wave anywhere in the paint, and the finished job shone like glass. I had plans the following day, so he said he would go ahead and remove all the masking tape and paper protecting the windows and replace all the trim, including the big four-inch chrome block letters that went across the front grill and spelled out FORD. My newly painted van would be completely ready for me by the time I got home.

When I returned that evening, he and Mom met me outside and excitedly pulled me by the hand to show me how sharp the van looked with all the chrome back in place. I walked around it with a huge smile on my face. It was beautiful. But Dad was behaving oddly. He was hopping around and chuckling, rubbing his hands together, barely keeping still. Something was up, and it had to be something other than the fact that the van was finally complete.

"What, Dad?" I asked, half amused and half dreading what had him so tickled.

"You'll see, you'll see!"

I looked to my mom for an answer. She just shrugged and rolled her eyes, then crossed her arms over her chest with that look that said, "You know your father."

"C'mon, c'mon . . . walk around again!" he implored me.

I slowly circled the van and came to the front once again, then saw what he had done. This was subtle, I'll give him that, but I wondered why nothing could ever just be normal.

He had reattached the individual letters that spelled out FORD so they read DORF instead. I pursed my lips and tried to keep the smile from my face, but when I turned to him and saw how deliriously happy he was that he had found this small way to be different without ignoring my pleas not to do anything too weird, I couldn't help but burst out laughing while he jumped up and down shouting, "Isn't that great! Isn't that great! The Dorfmobile!"

Mom and Dad did go boating together, and the *Virginia May or She May Not* proved to be a good little boat, although Mom was right: it was a bit large for them to handle on their own. They were in their seventies by this time, and eventually the outings became less frequent. When Jim and I had been married for about two years we decided we wanted to buy some property and move to the country. We had approached my parents about abandoning their island lifestyle and moving with us. They were enthusiastic about this proposition, and we even went to look at a few homes that might provide the space we would need to live together comfortably, when suddenly Mom was diagnosed with cancer. The progression was rapid, and in mind-numbing horror we watched her go from practically sprinting down the beach one day to being bedridden the next. Just three short months later, she was gone.

Together, my siblings and I, along with our father, lifted her ashes to the wind and let them fall upon the waters of the Gulf of Mexico. A few months after her death, Jim and I were slowly able to return to some semblance of normalcy and we proceeded with our plans to move from the crowded coastal town where we'd lived near my parents and buy a place in the country. It was decided that Dad would sell the home he and my mother had shared and move in with us. He wasn't taking care of himself since Mom passed away. He wouldn't, or couldn't, return to their bed and had been sleeping on the couch, and he was sliding further and further into a lonely depression. I was spending every evening at his house, doing his laundry, keeping the house clean, and making sure he ate. It seemed that a fresh new start was in order for all of us, and living together would be the perfect solution.

Moving and getting settled in our new home provided the distraction Dad needed to rise from his malaise. He and Jim worked side by side building shelves and workbenches as they went about setting up a shop in the huge outbuilding on our new property.

I busied myself getting the inside of the house in order, and was enjoying making new friends with all these people who owned horses. But every time I mentioned having one of my own someday Dad would only shake his head. He didn't quite understand my desire to have a horse. He thought it was going to be an awful expense and the commitment would tie us down. After several months of watching me struggle with Cody, he was thoroughly convinced that I had made a terrible mistake. Even after Cody and I had made great strides, he still felt I was being foolish for trying to ride such a high-spirited horse in my inexperience and was convinced the result would be disastrous.

"Why don't you sell that mare and find a horse you can ride safely? One that's trained." he asked one evening during dinner.

"Please, Dad, don't be like all the others who keep telling me to sell her. I will never part with her."

"But you can't even ride her! You bought a horse so you could go riding!"

"It's not her fault that I'm a lousy rider. Please try to understand. She's been through so much and has never found a reason to trust. She trusts me now, Dad. I can't just sell her off to an unknown fate."

He looked to Jim in frustration, only to receive a quiet look of equanimity.

"Well, what about getting a second horse?" Dad suggested. "One you can actually ride. This way, you could let Cody live her life in peace but still go riding like you dreamed about."

"That's a real nice idea, but a decent, well-trained horse costs about two grand. Two grand more than we have to spend on another horse," I answered.

Dad rose from the table and strode off to his bedroom. I glanced over at Jim, wondering what I said to make him leave so abruptly. Before either one of us had a chance to comment, he came back to the kitchen and stood beside Jim.

"Here," he said as he slapped his hand on the table. "You take this and make sure she gets a horse that's safe." There was a folded wad of bills beside Jim's plate.

"Dad . . . " I started to say.

"Now don't you argue about this," he interrupted. "I'm living here with you, and I know it's not always easy having an old man underfoot. Just let me do this, all right?"

"But Dad . . . " I started again.

"Why don't you just accept this money without argument?" He despised false humility and empty remarks, and always thought it odd that we don't simply say, "I'm thrilled you thought of me!" or "Thank you," instead of "You shouldn't have" or "No, this is our treat" when receiving a gift or being treated to dinner.

"Dad!" I exclaimed in frustration.

"What?" he snapped.

"I just want to know why *he* gets to hang onto the money?" I said, nodding at Jim. We all crumbled into laughter. I was getting another horse!

I had recently heard about a facility close by that bred Paint horses. Of course they would have youngsters for sale, but that's not what I was interested in buying. I did not have the knowledge or experience to work with an untrained two year old, although I was better armed in my search for a horse this time, and I knew exactly what I wanted. I didn't care about breed or sex, but I wanted a healthy, sound, well-trained, nine- to twelve-year-old calm trail horse. Someone told me they were selling a few of their older mares; maybe one of them would be perfect.

When I arrived I parked in the gravel and walked up to an office adjacent to a large barn. There was a woman just stepping through the door to go into the building, and she stopped when she saw me approach.

"Hi! Can I help you?" she asked.

"I hope so! I'm looking to buy a nice trail horse, and I heard you may have a few for sale," I answered.

"Yep, we sure do. C'mon through the barn and I'll show you around." She told me her name was Deb as she jumped off the porch and headed for the massive cross buck door to the barn. Deb flipped a latch, then leaned into the door with all her weight and pushed it open on its track. I could hear a radio playing and was startled by how loud it was as we entered the timber-frame structure. The aisle way formed a T, with a total of about twenty-five stalls along each side. But I'd never seen stalls quite like this. They were solid wood, with walls about eight feet high, including the front wall and the door. No windows, no gaps in the boards. You didn't know which stall housed a horse and which didn't until you were right in front of it. The interior of the barn was dark and gloomy, the only source of light filtering in through broken or warped boards that formed the exterior walls.

I looked around for the radio. I saw it hanging from a nail, about ten feet up on a post. Obviously the volume was never adjusted—you'd have to find a ladder to reach it. Deb had stepped up to one of the stalls and motioned for me to come close.

She leaned toward me and spoke loudly in my ear. "This is a real sweet mare." Deb opened the door and stood back to let me look. It was so dark in the stall I could barely see the horse. I thought it odd that the mare did not lift her head to the sound of the door opening, or even my approach. She appeared fit and healthy, but her behavior was lifeless and numb.

I stepped close to Deb and yelled, "What's with the radio? This is awful!"

"We keep it loud so the horses can't talk to each other," she responded without further explanation.

"What? What do you mean?" I had never heard anything so absurd about horse keeping in my life.

"It keeps them from forming bonds," she hollered back to me. "That's why the walls are so high, so they can't see each other. Less anxiety for our permanent ones because so many others come and go."

"Why don't you let your permanent ones form bonds?"

"Why bother," she shrugged. "Besides, what's permanent?"

This was incomprehensible to me, and I left there without seeing any other horses they had for sale. I couldn't stand to look in their lackluster eyes, for even though they were well fed and their physical needs were taken care of, to me they suffered abuse as severe as violent beating.

I began my search for a second horse full of upbeat anticipation, but as I trekked from barn to barn my excitement steadily turned to a weighty sorrow as I found out that my ignorance about horses in general when I'd brought Cody home more than a year before paled compared to how little I knew about the way so many horses are forced to live.

I encountered one woman who proudly showed me her immaculate barn. She told me she was able to work full-time, tend to her family and home, and still have the cleanest barn in the neighborhood.

"You've got to find ways to make your life easier," she told me as she indicated for me to look over the door of the stall. Her four horses, including the one for sale which I had come to see, were each hobbled and snub-tied to the wall so they couldn't move. Aside from when they were being worked, her horses were forced to stand like this for sixteen to eighteen hours a day, with just a few hours of turnout in the morning and a few at night.

"This way they potty in one place. Makes cleanup a breeze!" she proudly announced. I felt nauseated and left there with a heavy sadness.

I heard about a very well-trained dressage horse that was ready for retirement but still very fit. I knew nothing about dressage and he was older than I intended on buying, but I decided it wouldn't hurt to go look at him. The woman who owned the horse kept him at home rather than a boarding facility, and I phoned her to set up a day we could meet. She lived in an exclusive equestrian neighborhood. Her tree-lined driveway offered an idyllic scene, horses peacefully grazing in the pasture.

"Why are you selling him?" I asked. We were standing at the fence line watching her two horses.

"He just can't perform like I need him to anymore. He's sound and very healthy, but I need an athlete. He's seventeen now. Time for him to take it easy."

"How long have you had him?"

She sighed deeply, then said, "Fifteen years."

"Wow," I said.

"Yeah, it'll be hard to say good-bye to him. And hard on him, as well, I imagine. Aside from where he was born, this is the only home he's ever known."

"Hmm," I muttered, hearing the sadness in the woman's voice and feeling bad for her.

"I'm bringing home a little pony that a friend's giving me to be a companion to the new boy I just bought," she said, nodding toward the big bay gelding.

"Why don't you keep your older fella as his companion," I asked.

She looked at me like I had a screw loose and replied with an ironic chuckle, "Because I'll never ride him again, and I can get fifteen hundred bucks for him."

I understand that we all have different agendas and what motivates one person will not move another, but as I looked around at this woman's half-million-dollar home it was clear that she did not need the money. What would she be sacrificing if she provided a peaceful and dignified retirement for this horse who had given her his very best for fifteen years? She had the opportunity to return an amazing gift to him for all he had done if she could only find it in her heart to make a commitment to this deserving horse.

My quest for a horse would finally take me to the classifieds in the newspaper. One day, going down the column of horses for sale, there he was—the description of my perfect horse. He sounded exactly like what I was looking for and I immediately reached for the phone. The woman who answered was very friendly. She told me her name was Janie and we ended up talking for quite a while. But what struck me as odd was that she asked me more questions about how her horse would be living should I decide to buy him than I asked her about the horse.

"I'll tell you right up front," Janie said, "we won't sell him to just anybody. And before anything gets settled, my husband and I will want to come see your place."

I was stunned. All these weeks of looking at horses for sale, and not one person had ever asked me one single question about how or where their horse would be living. "I've got no problem with that," I cheerfully replied.

Jim decided to go with me when I went to look at Janie's horse, and Janie and her husband were out by their barn when we pulled in the drive. You could tell that someone had a passion for gardening and flowers. The grounds of their home were lush with vibrant color, and interesting displays caught your eye everywhere you looked.

Introductions were made all around. Janie's husband, Tom, was a big man like Jim, and aside from a physical likeness they had similar personalities and seemed to hit it off immediately.

Janie was a small woman with a pixie haircut that suited her perfectly. She had the most beautiful smile, which reached all the way to her twinkling eyes.

"Well, let's go see the horses!" she said.

We walked to the fence line and she called out, "Dira! Jordy! Strutter! C'mon, babies!"

From the pasture around the side of the house came a pounding of hooves. Suddenly, three of the most gorgeous horses I had ever seen rounded the corner and ran directly to our side. "There's my babies," Janie cooed. They clambered around her vying for Janie's attention while she scratched manes and kissed muzzles. These horses were bright and alive with a pervading vibrancy that spoke of the love and care they received as well as the way they were allowed to live—like horses.

I stood watching, tears stinging my eyes. I had seen so many disturbing situations the last few weeks. In barn after barn it was commonplace and normal to ignore—even worse, destroy—a horse's spirit and emotional well-being. It was extraordinary to me now to witness this celebration of the equine life force. For those who would never know the heights they could reach with their horses if they would only set their spirits free, I could only feel sorry.

The four of us, Tom, Janie, Jim, and I, talked for several hours that day. They invited us into their home and we chatted over cold beers in the friendly ambiance of their kitchen. We learned that Tom and Janie were moving to North Carolina and embarking on a new adventure in life. They were taking their mare, Naadira, with them, but the situation would prevent them from moving all three horses. It was clearly breaking their hearts to sell Strut and Jordy, and they were making every effort to ensure good permanent homes for the two geldings.

My close friend Tommi actually ended up buying Jordy and still owns him. And with the money my father gave us I purchased Strut. He remains to this day a genuine friend and gives me remarkable equine companionship. His calm and gentle confidence provided me the opportunity to improve my riding skills, and Strut and I have enjoyed years of trail riding together. This chance meeting through an ad in the paper brought us another very relevant gift—a lifelong friendship with Janie and Tom.

We had settled into a pleasant life at our home on five acres in the country. Cody and Strut had become fast friends, and my dad was thrilled that I had a safe horse to ride. My dad had always been extremely active and vital, but he was going on eighty years old now and was slowing down considerably. He had been diagnosed with prostate cancer the year my mother died, and we recently learned that it had metastasized to his bone. He had initially expressed a deep fear of dying, and then an ensuing sadness as he pondered all the unfinished projects and life experiences left undone.

"I wish I had flown on the Concorde," he said to me one day. He was very ill at this point and had trouble getting out of bed. I had him propped up on his pillows and he was spearing with a toothpick chunks of watermelon I had just cut up for him. We were never a family to avoid difficult subjects. I never made light of his approaching death, speaking as if it wasn't going to happen. I was sitting on the end of his bed, waiting for him to finish so I could take the dish from his shaky hands.

"You never know, Dad, maybe this next adventure will be more exciting than flying on the Concorde," I told him through a sad smile.

He looked up at me and slowly nodded. "Yeah, maybe it will be."

One afternoon Dad wanted to come and sit in the warm sun. Jim and I placed some pillows in his favorite lawn chair and helped him out to the yard. Once we had him settled in I decided to saddle Strut and show Dad how well we were doing. Jim was close by in the driveway waxing his truck. I brought Strut into the yard, and speaking loudly and dramatically as if through a microphone, I announced, "And now, for the main event! The amazing Strutter!" We were the main attraction of a traveling show that drew crowds from miles around. Strut and I would trot little circles around Dad's chair, then I would ask Strut to stop directly in front of him and back up in a straight line. What a grand time I had showing off. Strut complied like a champion with everything I asked, making me appear to be a much better rider than I actually was. How Dad laughed and laughed that day.

"Look at you! Look at you!" he kept exclaiming. "This is great! Boy, oh, boy! This is just great!"

After about a half hour I could see that Dad was getting tired. He was already falling asleep as Strut and I made our exit. When I was coming back into the yard from around the barn after unsaddling and grooming Strut, I glanced up and was startled to see Dad's face. He was prone in his lawn chair, and he looked morbidly pale as his eyes eerily searched the clouds. He weakly called out, "Jim!"

I was immobilized with fear. I thought he was dying. My hand was over my mouth as my eyes darted to Jim. He dropped the rag he was using to wax his truck and quietly said, "What is it, Rex?"

Dad let out a deep sigh and replied, "Oh, good. You can hear me, and I can hear you, so I must not be dead."

"What are you talking about, Dad?" I asked from behind his chair.

"There. I thought they were coming to get me." Slowly, he lifted his right hand off his chest and pointed upward. We followed its direction and saw a flock of vultures circling high overhead. I looked over at Jim, then back to Dad. We all burst into a wild fit of laughter. That became our little joke. Leave it to Rex Foster to depart this life on the wings of vultures rather than angels.

A few days later, Dad became completely bedridden. My work as a firefighter and EMT prepared me for what was happening to him physically, but I was not prepared emotionally. He had not managed to eat that day, but I made him a small milkshake and it soothed his stomach. I sat curled up in the lounge chair in his bedroom that evening. We were watching TV together, or rather the TV was on. I kept the volume turned all the way down and we both absently stared in its direction, not talking. Not talking at all. As darkness came I didn't get up to turn on a lamp, and still, we just sat quietly, each enveloped in our thoughts.

I was keenly aware that my father was dying. I'm sure he knew it as well, and the confounding paradox of life and death revealed itself to me as he and I sat in the blue glow of the television set. I felt at once deeply connected to him yet displaced, for he would take this journey alone. I was sad for my five siblings that they were not here to say good-bye, and yet on some levels I was glad that they were not and that I was given this time alone with our father. And I was changed forever in the way I perceived him.

For here was a man who throughout his entire life had actively made his presence known. He was opinionated and vocal. He dressed like a dandy and was at times cocky and egotistical. He enthusiastically took on City Hall at every opportunity. He unabashedly yelled out his support of the hero in movie houses. He believed in living every minute and taking a bite out of life. I expected him to face death with a clenched fist shook toward the heavens as he railed at the Fates that he should be taken from this life.

But perhaps because he did live life so fully he was able to almost appreciatively accept death and step into its fold with quiet dignity.

I could see the clock on his nightstand and it was nearing midnight. He appeared to be sleeping but must have felt my eyes on him and turned his head to look toward the chair where I still sat. He lifted his hand and motioned me to his bedside. I uncurled myself from the lounge chair and went to him. He was lying on his side as I approached but rolled onto his back when I reached his bed. He took my hand, and I sandwiched his with my free hand, our fingers entwined. I stood over him for several minutes and we simply looked into each other's eyes, yet still did not speak. Still did not utter a word. There was no gnawing need to make some sort of affirmation of our feelings or validate our relationship. Our mutual silence brought about a soothing consummation to his parting of this life that words would only sully.

My eyes blurred and I blinked several times, my tears falling upon our clasped hands. He smiled up at me then and nodded, and the accepting, peaceful look on his face comforted me. It was as though he was telling me he was okay with this, he was ready. Through my tears, I weakly nodded and smiled back at him and squeezed his hand. We remained that way for several more minutes. Then I went back to my chair and dozed. Rex quietly passed away before morning's light.

My father had lived with Jim and me for five years, and in the months following his death we went about creating a life without his presence. I returned to my job as a firefighter and EMT but had lost heart for the work. Florida is a retirement state, and naturally the mortality rate is high. After experiencing the profound and dignified way my father left this life, I became less than enthusiastic about responding to the frantic 911 calls by the family members of a bedridden elderly person in their eighties or nineties who was dying. All I could think about was how people in our society relentlessly cling to life at all costs, denying themselves and their loved ones the final gift of peace and serenity as we burst in with our medical boxes and respiratory bags and defibrillators while everyone is yelling and crying for us to "do something." The noise and confusion became almost obscene to me, a violation, and I wanted to tell them all to just let their dying loved ones be. Hold them close to you and tell them you love them, but let them be. We are strangers to you, I wanted to tell the frantic families. We don't belong here at the death of your loved ones. . . .

I had markedly suppressed my grief at the loss of my mother. I felt I had to be strong for my dad. And now, I was holding back my grief for him. I don't know why I did this, but it was not a conscious decision. This pent-up anguish, coupled with the dissatisfaction and frustration I felt at work, culminated in an extremely stressful time for me.

An acquaintance of mine had approached me several times in the past about buying Cody from me. Barbara owned a boarding and training facility on forty-five beautiful acres about an hour from our place. She felt it was a shameful waste for Cody to languish in my pasture and never be ridden. Shortly after Dad had died we ran into each other at a mutual friend's house and she brought the subject up again.

"I've got a new program starting for experienced fifteen- to eighteen-year-old girls. Cody would be a perfect lesson horse," she told me.

"I don't know, Barb. I really don't want to sell her."

"You've just been saying that you really went through a lot with your dad and you're in a bit of overload. Why not lighten your chores at home and let me take her for a while? Nothing permanent. I'll send you a check every month to lease her, just through this next season," she said.

With a deep sense of foreboding, I agreed to Barb's offer and she came with her trailer the following weekend. As I stood in the driveway saying good-bye to my precious girl, Strut stood at the fence watching wide-eyed as Barb walked his beloved companion up the ramp. When Cody disappeared into the depths of the trailer, Strut stomped his front hooves and let out an ear-piercing scream. Cody answered his call and instantly became agitated as she searched for an escape.

"Oh, Barb, I don't think I want to do this. I don't know what I was thinking. Strut and Cody are very attached," I exclaimed.

Barb walked over to me and placed her hand on my arm. "Honey, I've had horses for thirty years. They get over it."

"But why are we always doing things to them that they need to get over?" I was close to tears and Barb gently squeezed my arm.

"Let's just give this a try. I'll call you this evening and let you know how she's settled in, and you can come see her anytime you want. Now, the sooner I get going, the sooner both Cody and your other horse will calm down."

Strut was running back and forth along the fence line and he'd already worked himself into a sweat. Cody was screaming over and over and pawing the wall of the trailer.

"All right! Just go!" I told her.

As Barb pulled out of our driveway, Strut ran in a panic along the fence trying to stay with the trailer. When he reached the property line and could go no further he stood there as if in shock, rigid and straining against the boards, answering Cody's screams. Barb turned the corner and we could no longer see the trailer, but for several minutes we could still hear Cody screaming. I felt like I'd been punched in the stomach.

For the remainder of the day Strut paced the front fence line. Periodically he would stop and look down the road and yell a heart-wrenching call for Cody. By evening he had not relaxed his vigil for her return and ignored my calls to come for his dinner. As the sun was setting I walked out with Strut's grain and stood in front of him holding the bucket while he ate, but he never took his eyes from the last place he saw that trailer.

"I'm so sorry, buddy," I told him. "This was a huge mistake." I started to cry and wearily set the bucket on the ground. Strut didn't seem to care that it was still half full of grain. I buried my face in his powerful neck and sobbed. I cried for him, for Cody, for my mom and dad . . . and for me. This was the cleansing release I needed so badly, and when I was through I at once felt at peace about the loss of my parents.

I would look back on this later and forgive myself for allowing Cody to be taken from her home. But the next few days I still grappled with my newly developing notions and knowledge about horses. Was I being overly concerned, placing so much emphasis on their emotional well-being? Was I wrong to do this? Why didn't it ever seem to matter to anyone else—even people who were kind and conscientious? Barb was a wonderful person. I had been out to her place many times. She was never harsh or rough with her horses and believed in many of the same things I did, which is why I even considered letting her take Cody. But even she disregarded the torment both Cody and Strut endured by this separation we forced upon them. Why didn't it matter?

Barb had called the first evening to let me know that Cody had been turned out into a two-acre paddock with lots of grass. She was alone for now but could see the other horses, and Barb assured me she was fine. The afternoon of the third day, she called again. "What are you doing tomorrow?" Barb wanted to know. "I was wondering if you could come out."

"Is everything all right?" I asked.

"Yes, everything's fine. I just thought you might like to see Cody," she said.

"I'm free today. I could come out right now," I told her.

"That's good with me. I'll see you in about an hour or so," she said.

I grabbed the straw cowboy hat that I always wore to protect my face from the sun and headed right out. I planned to tell Barb that I wished to renege on this deal we had made. I wanted Cody back home. I vigorously rehearsed my speech during the drive but feared this was not going to be easy. I was sure by the tone of her voice that she had asked me to come out so I could see for myself that Cody had settled in nicely and wasn't giving Strut, or the life she had with me, a second thought.

But I didn't care about any of that. No one would ever convince me that horses don't form genuine bonds with their pasture mates, their home, and the people who care for them. I was furious at myself for doing something I swore I never would. I'd betrayed Cody's trust by not listening to my heart.

At this point the agreement for Barb to lease Cody had been verbal. No money had changed hands, and no papers had been signed. I would approach this in a friendly way and hoped Barb would agree. But whether she did or not, Cody was coming back home—period. I just prayed this would not destroy the growing friendship between Barb and me. At the same time, I prepared for a fight.

Barb's lush property was spattered with enormous old oak trees. She had four good-sized pastures along each side of the driveway, which took you directly to the twelve-stall barn. If you made a right just past the office that was attached to the barn, the driveway then looped around a low swampy area with a remarkably beautiful stand of cypress trees and back around to Barb's house. I stopped in front of the barn and went to find Barb.

I found her in the office sitting at her desk tending to some paperwork. She smiled and waved for me to come in. "Did you see Cody as you came in?" she asked.

"No . . . " I answered.

"Oh, she's right out in the second paddock." Barb rose from her chair and leaned across her desk to point out the window. "Why don't you go ahead and walk out to her? I'll just finish up this one thing I'm working on and join you two in a minute."

I nodded and turned to walk outside, still determined to take Cody home. I was upset for Strut, who still had not settled down. I was drastically disappointed in myself, and I was nervous and worried about how Barb would react when I told her I had changed my mind. But most of all, I was heartbroken for Cody.

As I approached the paddock where she was grazing, I could see her off in the far corner, her head down and her back to me. I climbed up on the bottom rail of the board fencing and called out to her the same way I always called her for dinner, "Cody! C'mon!"

Her head shot up to the sky, but she didn't turn around. She stood immobilized, and I wondered what she was doing. I climbed through the boards and walked a few feet, then called again, "Cody! C'mon!" Now she reeled around and stared in my direction. I was crying now and couldn't wait to touch her and smell her wonderful smell. I started to run towards her, and through my tears I yelled again, "C'mon girl!" Cody's eyes were wide and she let out a loud whinny, then suddenly she tossed her head and galloped as hard as she could to meet me.

When she reached my side I put my arms around her neck. "I'm so sorry, Cocoa," I told her. "You're coming home, baby. I'm so, so sorry." Cody was nickering in that low throaty baffled sound that horses make, *herrherrherr*. Then she started pushing my shoulder with her head, trying to get me to face her. When I complied and stepped back so I was at her head, she leaned down to my mouth and rapidly blew through her nostrils. I blew back so she could smell my breath—this is the equine equivalent of a handshake.

We stood saying hello for about five minutes. I was exhilarated. I stopped crying, wiping my tears with her mane. When I looked up, Barb was standing at the fence line.

"I was watching from my office," Barb said. She looked down at the ground, then sighed and shook her head. "I have something I want to tell you."

I walked over to where she stood, perplexed by the look on her face and the tears shimmering in *her* eyes. Cody followed me, trying to keep physical contact.

"Melanie, I have had daily, intimate interaction with horses for over thirty years and I've never seen anything like this."

"I don't know what you mean," I said.

"Well, I didn't want to say anything on the phone, but we have not been able to get near Cody for three days. Even when we've tried bribing her with grain, she hasn't let us within ten feet of her. And I didn't want to say anything till I saw how she reacted to you, but I have to tell you, this is extraordinary."

I tipped my head back to look at Cody. She was standing with her chest against my back, her muzzle touching the side of my head. "It shouldn't be, Barb. It should be ordinary and natural—don't you think?"

Barb smiled at me and nodded. "You're very blessed to have what she feels for you. Take her home, Mel, and don't ever part with her."

My father had been on my mind almost constantly these last few months since his passing. How does a parent bequeath values and inspiration to his child? What legacy would I carry forward as a result of being raised by this man? He was not perfect. He had warts and baggage like everybody else. But he was also a unique and remarkable individual. How would I honor that? Something he used to say to me was at the forefront of my thoughts the entire ride back home from my encounter with Barb: "Everything you experience, good and bad, is all part of the rich fabric of life. Use these experiences to make the world better."

That evening, Jim and I were standing outside watching the sun set. He was sitting up on the top rail of the fence. I had something I wanted to tell him. I'd never been more sure of anything in my life than of what I was about to say, and I had to word it right. It wouldn't work if there was even a hint of opposition from him or one bit of hesitation. This had to be something we were in one-hundred-percent, total agreement about.

"Jim . . . " I started.

"Hmm." He tilted his head to look down where I stood with my chin resting on my hands along the top rail of the fence.

I stood up and looked toward the rosy glow of the setting sun.

"You know that quote I love by Marjory Stoneman Douglas?" I said, my eyes still averted from his. "The one where at the end of the quote she says, 'Count your blessings by the lives you've touched'?"

"Mmm, I think so," he nodded.

"I've been thinking about my dad a lot lately, and that quote. I don't want to come to the end of my life, whenever that may be, and look back over my time here and wonder what I did to make a difference." I stopped and took a deep breath, then looked up at him. "I want to make a difference in the lives of horses, Jim, lots of horses. I want to have a sanctuary for any horse that needs us that's been abused, neglected, abandoned, or forgotten. A place where they can live out their lives in peace and dignity."

I looked away from him, back to the setting sun, and waited

for his response. He released a pensive sigh as he surveyed our five-acre parcel. Then I felt his eyes on me once again and turned my head to look at him. He blinked a few times, then gave me that little one-sided smile of his and said, "We'll have to get more land . . ." ♘

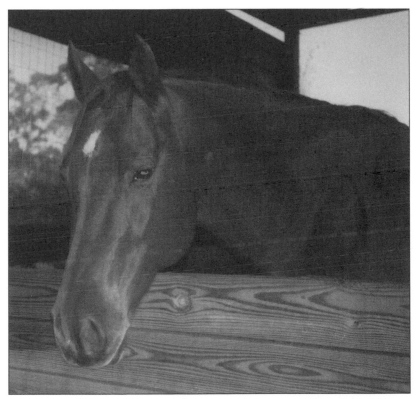

Strut quietly dozing after eating his supper as the sun goes down behind him.

Dusty

As I lifted my foot to put it in the stirrup, all my apprehension suddenly disappeared. I'd had trouble getting to sleep the previous night, once I'd made the decision to ride him for the first time. Morning had come and I still wasn't sure this was such a bright idea.

At this point I was very proud of my accomplishments in communicating with horses from the ground. Strut and Cody were perfectly settled in now and had formed a close bond. My experiences with them revealed to me over and over that my chosen method of working with hurting horses reached them emotionally and touched their spirit at a level most never see.

But one lingering concern as I mounted this new horse was that my riding skills still left much to be desired. The entire time I'd been grooming him I'd kept wishing Jim were home in case Dusty tried to catapult me into the next county. "I'll just see how he reacts to being tacked up," I told myself. Standing in front of him holding the saddle, I let him smell the leather. And just to break the tension I asked, "Wha'cha think, pal? Wanna give it a go?" He seemed unconcerned as I walked to his side and gently lifted the saddle to his back.

I turned to pick up the girth and in the split second that my back was turned he had reached around, grabbed the stirrup in his teeth and almost succeeded in pulling the saddle clean off his back. I laughed, as this was typical of his "into everything" behavior.

After finishing with the saddle, I removed his halter and picked up the bridle to set the bit at his mouth. He took it like he had been doing so every day for the past year rather than just the opposite—for he hadn't had a bit in his mouth for at least that long. He kept his head lowered as I fastened the straps of the bridle. I then pulled his forelock out from beneath the leather and cupped my hands over both his eyes. He loved when I did this and closed his eyes gently while letting out a big sigh. I smiled at his response, the memories of the very first time I rubbed his eyes flooding my mind.

But now there was business to do. I led him to the mounting block, patting his neck while he walked calmly with his head down. Standing in front of him, talking softly and rubbing his forehead, I tried to predict how he was going to behave by the look in his eye. He put his nose against my belt and gave me a nudge, as if to say, "C'mon, let's go!" I took a slow deep breath, gave another tug to my helmet strap, and put the reins over his head.

The horse I was preparing to ride is a huge, strapping, gray Thoroughbred who had come to us more than a year before. At that time he was emaciated and broken down, both physically and emotionally. He was so sullen and bedraggled—as though he'd been ridden hard on a two-week trail—that I decided to name him Dusty. How we ended up together is a story that began during the month I'd spent searching for a second horse and had found Strut. My month-long search for Strut had taken me to an entirely different place in my education about horses and I had vowed I would make a difference.

Early one Saturday morning, my friend Kera called. She wanted to know if I would go with her to look at a horse she was thinking about buying. Kera had heard about a place near us that rested and rehabilitated Thoroughbreds off the track. Sometimes, for a variety of reasons, the owners of these horses in recovery decide it's not worth transporting them back to wherever they came from and tell the people running the facility to sell them.

While Kera looked at the horse she had come to see, I wandered down the row of stalls. The barn and grounds were fairly clean and in good repair, with probably forty horses on the property. Most were confined to stalls and appeared to be fairly young. I soon noticed that their youthful exuberance, restrained as it was, had turned ugly. These youngsters were using every means they could to relieve their boredom. Some were mindlessly weaving back and forth, some were chewing the wood of their stalls, and others had developed the habit of cribbing or wind sucking, when a horse places his front teeth on a hard surface and then pulls back and repeatedly takes in gulps of air.

Many people think this habit will cause colic so they put what is known as a cribbing collar on the horse. This prevents him from using his neck muscles to pull back and gulp air. I noticed several horses with these tight, heavy leather straps in place around their throats. But this notion of wind sucking causing colic has been dispelled by most veterinary professionals. Just as some of us are fidgety, or bite our fingernails, or develop the habit of smoking, certain horses need to fidget. These horses are already high-strung and may very well be prone to colic, but placing a collar around their necks and denying them the release they need may, in fact, bring about a stress-related bout of colic. Oftentimes, simply allowing this horse some freedom and companionship can greatly reduce his stress. He may still crib, but he at least knows some contentment.

It was depressing to walk along the aisle way seeing all these youngsters stored like inanimate objects in a warehouse. But when I came to the end of the barn the feeling in the pit of my stomach worsened. I looked out the back and noticed a very small, skinny, gray horse off in a paddock standing alone. He was absolutely motionless, his head hanging almost to the ground. Watching for a moment, I noticed that he couldn't put weight on his left front leg. Horses are always flicking their ears or swishing their tails, but this poor boy was oblivious to the flies. He was sullen and still, as though he'd given up. I swallowed hard and turned away.

I walked back to the barn and returned to Kera standing with the man who was showing her the horse for sale. She was holding the horse's lead rope and asked me what I thought. "He's a handsome boy," I answered, then turned to the man.

"What's the story on the little gray out back?" I asked him.

He looked at me for a second, probably wondering why I was interested and how he should answer me, for the little horse was clearly being neglected. Kera looked at me too. I'm sure she heard my tone of voice, concern mingled with anger. Although Kera loves animals as much as I do, she sometimes wishes I would mind my own business.

"Well, he'll be going for a drive soon," was all the man would say. We left shortly thereafter.

On the way home Kera talked about the horse she was thinking about buying, but I wasn't really listening. I couldn't stop thinking about the little gray. Over the next few days his tormented image kept crowding my mind. I didn't quite know what to do, so I did nothing. I'd learned that animal control would not get involved if there was food and water available and the facility was in good repair. This was certainly the case here, and all the owners would have to say about the skinny gray was that he'd been ill. So for a few days, I fretted about how I could intervene on his behalf.

Then Kera called to say that she had decided to purchase the horse she had looked at and asked if I wanted to go with her to pick him up. She was going to be leaving in a few minutes, just as soon as she hitched up her trailer. I silently hoped the gray was still alive. Without hesitation I told her I would join her.

While Kera backed her trailer in and exchanged money and papers with the man, I walked out back to see if the gray was still there. He was, and in fact it looked like he had not moved an inch. This time I walked out to the fence line.

He did not lift his head, but I saw his brow move as he shifted his eye in my direction. I set my hands on the top rail and softly said, "What happened to you, fella?" Slowly he turned his head at the sound of my voice so both eyes were on me, his nose practically dragging on the ground. His eyes seemed to implore: "Do something . . . anything . . . somehow get me out of here or mercifully end my misery, but do something. Just please don't walk away." In that instant I knew with all my heart that I would indeed do something. Somehow I would get him out of there.

I walked back to the barn and found Kera standing in the aisle with the horse she had just bought. The man was nowhere around.

"Where's the guy?" I whispered to her.

"He's in the office finishing up the paperwork. What's wrong?"

"Kera, that emaciated gray horse is still here. We need to get him out of here," I said.

"Okay. How?"

"I'm gonna see if he'll just give him to me. Maybe let us take him right now," I told her as I walked past her and headed toward the office.

The small office was located at the front of the barn and I could see through a window that the man was sitting at a desk. I quietly rapped once against the closed door, then turned the knob and poked my head inside.

"You got a minute?" I asked.

He glanced at me, looked back to the papers on his desk and said with distraction, "Sure."

"Um, I'm sorta taken with the little gray horse out back," I began.

He leaned back in his chair and pushed away from the desk to turn and look at me. "Uh huh," he muttered, as he laced his fingers together across his stomach.

"Well, he doesn't look like he's doing real good. Would you let me just take him off your hands?"

"Sure, you can take him off my hands," he laughed. "For a price."

"He's nothing but skin and bones, and he's injured besides. You're not gonna be able to sell him."

"Well, here's a news flash for ya, sweetie" he said as he stood up and collected the papers for Kera's new horse. "That skin and bones out there will fetch me about four hundred dollars at the slaughterhouse. You want him, that's what you can give me."

Horses going to slaughter is a fact of life, and it's probably not going to go away. The European market for horse meat is and always will be strong. While Americans may find this repulsive, it is not our place to judge another culture on what it deems suitable for the dinner plate. We can, however, reduce the numbers of horses killed for this purpose by making a responsible decision to have a veterinarian kindly euthanize our companion horses who are no longer able to give—due to illness, injury, or age.

My ethic holds me to believe that this is the way it should be, and many horses are put to rest in this manner by loving owners who are thankful to their equine friends for all they've given. I can not imagine allowing one of my own horses to be loaded onto a stranger's trailer and then simply turning away, as if the culmination of our lives together meant nothing more than a cold ride to the slaughterhouse. When the quality of life for our horses has declined and it's time that we let go, for me to sleep at night, my hand smoothing their mane must be the final thing they feel, my voice whispering "Go easy" the last thing they hear once our vet arrives to administer euthanasia.

But it is unreasonable to think that all horses will meet so kind a fate when you consider the thousands and thousands of unwanted horses generated yearly by everything from the racing industry all the way down to irresponsible breeding and callous owners trying to get the last dollar out of an elderly backyard pony that the children no longer ride.

And so for those horses who fall into that unfortunate unwanted category and do end up at the slaughterhouse, we as cognizant, reasonable, and, I hope, compassionate human beings have the responsibility to make sure the process is carried out in a humane manner. And this includes transportation of these unwanted horses to the plant.

I did not argue with the little gray's caretaker or tell him that this horse would never survive the grueling trailer ride to Texas, which has the slaughterhouse closest to Florida that renders horses. I did not tell him that the horse simply did not have the strength. I was sure that the hauler would more than likely pull into the rendering plant with a dead horse on the floor of his stock trailer, and he would not get a dime. I was actually doing him a favor by taking the gray off his hands. But I did not tell him any of this. I only wanted the horse away from him, and away from this awful place, and so I paid the man four hundred dollars.

Three hours after I'd hauled the injured gray to our property, my vet was at his side. Aside from the obvious malnutrition and extreme depression; numerous scars, cuts, and lacerations over his entire body; and chipped teeth from his abusers using a stud chain in his mouth to control him, X-rays would also reveal several hairline fractures and a bone chip in his left knee. There was stress damage to his right foot, plus the scars of pin-firing were up and down all four legs. He was just two years old.

While very supportive, my vet warned that the road to recovery would be a long one. I had already accepted that commitment. After the vet left us I led Dusty to a freshly bedded stall. Every step was agony for him as he threw his head to make forward motion possible.

Once in the stall he just stood with his head down. A mountain lion could have been in the rafters and he wouldn't have cared. I had never in my life seen such a sullen horse. I tried to give him chunks of apple, but he wouldn't even open his mouth. I removed his halter, all the while talking softly and moving calmly as I began to rub his forehead and all around his ears. His head was hanging so low it was easier for me if I knelt down.

My face was very close to his as I sat on my knees, and he just stared at me, never taking his eyes from mine. I continued to rub his face and softly tell him he was okay now, no one would hurt him ever again. Finally he let out a huge sigh, started to salivate and work his mouth, and then he closed his eyes.

I stopped talking then but kept rubbing his neck, face, and ears, my cheek resting against his as I gently hugged his head. After about fifteen minutes he opened his eyes slightly and then without pawing or circling he dropped to his good knee and tried to lie down. His body trembled with the effort it took for one leg to bear all his weight and I was worried about how he would get back up, but he clearly needed to get off his feet. I had scooted backwards on my knees to get out of his way and watched as he lay flat and let out an enormous shuddering sigh, and then shut his eyes.

It had been an emotionally exhausting day for me, but he was obviously way beyond exhausted, both physically and mentally. I decided we both needed to rest and stood to leave, but when I put my hand on the stall latch his head shot up and he nickered so softly it was more like a hoarse whisper.

I turned back to look at him and was suddenly overcome by the sight of him—this beaten, starved, exhausted little baby who had suffered so much at the hands of humans, yet wanted me to stay with him. I went back to him and knelt down. There were tears in my eyes as I stroked his neck and eased his head back down. I couldn't even talk to soothe him with my voice . . . it felt like there was a vise around my throat.

As he lay flat once more, he kept opening one eye to look at me and then it would flutter closed. He was so tired, but he wouldn't stop looking at me, as if he was afraid I would leave if he fell asleep. Finally I cupped my hand over his eye and slowly rubbed downward until his eye stayed closed and he fell into a deep, deep sleep.

I couldn't bring myself to leave, so I just leaned back against the wall of the stall, my arms wrapped around my drawn-up knees, dirt, tears, and pine shavings smeared all over my face. I decided he needed to know where my heart was and deserved to have me there when he woke up. He slept deeply for about an hour and a half. I may have dozed too, but as I sat watching him I asked myself how anyone could allow—or even worse, inflict— the atrocious abuse Dusty had been through. I was ashamed of myself for turning away from him that first day, but thankful that he was here with us now.

The evenings were my favorite time of day during Dusty's recovery. We would come to him after all the other chores were finished and stand with him at his stall to watch the sun go down. He would rest his head on my shoulder, sighing contentedly while I rubbed his face and ears and Jim tirelessly contributed to easing his boredom, spending long periods of time scratching his back and hind end. Dusty would stand with his head in the air, his eyes half closed and his lip curled in ecstasy, leaning into Jim's big hands as he worked up and down his back.

My friend Tommi, a licensed equine massage therapist, had taught me some techniques to help Dusty relax and deal with the tensions of being idle. We spent hours massaging his legs—especially his good one, as it bore all his weight—until his broken knee started to heal. Before we went in for the night, I always ended the evening by helping Dusty to completely settle in. I would rub his face and ears until he'd put his head down against my chest. Then I would cup my hands over his eyes and rub them closed. He just loved this, and it made him drowsy.

There were many evenings when I could get him to lie right down. I would sit on the floor with him and hold his head in my lap. He would stare up at me while I told him how much I loved him and how thankful I was that he was here with us and was a part of this family.

As Dusty's health improved, a personality emerged that made the abuse even harder to grasp. He became interested in everything around him and was willing to listen and please. In what seemed like no time at all, right before our very eyes, he was transformed from a despondent shell of a horse into an incredibly vibrant and deliriously happy boy who demanded our attention.

Dusty had to spend several months confined to his stall while his knee was healing, with just some hand grazing three or four times a day. This was very difficult for him as he became easily bored and looked for anything to break the monotony. We provided him with safe horse toys and plenty of hay and spent an incredible amount of one-on-one time with him. But these diversions weren't enough for this energetic big guy, and he was constantly into one thing after the other.

I don't believe that horses are capable of plotting or are "out to get us," even in fun. But I have a clear notion that Dusty could reason about the pranks he pulled, as well as the desired outcome.

Numerous times during the day I would go into Dusty's stall to pick out the manure. On this particular day he casually watched me come into his stall with my plastic rake. He was just standing there, not paying much attention to me, seemingly minding his own business while I chattered away to him. I was standing with my back to him, busily cleaning up his piles, when he slowly strolled over to me. I was oblivious to his mischievous intentions as he leaned down and touched my hair with his mouth. Suddenly, he dropped a huge mouthful of water down my back!

Now maybe he didn't know what he was doing. Maybe this was just some sort of coincidental behavior that had nothing to do with him gleefully watching me bolt upright in shock. Maybe it wasn't pure delight I saw in his eyes as he backed away from me and dropped his head to resume eating hay as if nothing had happened. Maybe he thought I looked hot and was trying to be kind and helpful by cooling me off. Maybe. But after that day no one would ever convince me that horses can't smile.

I did, however, get in the habit of sticking my finger in his mouth upon entering his stall to make him open up and reveal any surprises he may be holding. It only took me a few weeks and several back drenches to learn to do that.

One day I was working around the barn and noticed Jim standing near Dusty's stall, looking a little lost.

"What are you doing?" I asked.

"I'm gonna go work on that cross fencing, but I can't find my gloves."

"They were right there on that shelf," I said, pointing to the ledge.

"Yeah, I know, but they're not here." His voice trailed off and we both turned to look at Dusty, who was standing at his stall door listening to this exchange.

"I don't think he can reach that shelf, Jim. They must be around here somewhere."

Just then Dusty turned away from us, breaking eye contact. If he could have whistled he would have strolled away while a casual tune resonated in his wake.

"Mmm hmm," nodded Jim. "I'll just *bet* he can't reach that shelf." Jim slid the latch aside and walked into Dusty's stall. He looked around for a moment, then shuffled his feet along the edge of the stall, displacing the shavings. There were his gloves, stuck in a corner and buried under six inches of fluffy bedding. They were unrecognizable as gloves anymore, for Dusty had chewed them into a slobbery mass of leather. But there they were.

Dusty also loved to steal hats off our heads. He would grab one and then hold his head high in the air, the hat clenched tightly in his teeth. If we weren't fast enough, he would gaily throw it in the air and paw it into oblivion after it landed on the floor of his stall.

When Dusty was finally able to function in a herd situation I put him with my other horses. He had filled out into a huge, graceful, and muscular teenager. I couldn't help but think, as I looked at his powerful hindquarters and massive leg muscles, that if he hadn't been run into the ground at such a young age he would have been an incredible athlete. He was solid as a rock and had the heart to be a winner.

Dusty was thrilled to have some equine pals and quickly established himself as the dominant horse—yet he still seems to prefer human company. After mealtime, as the others wander off to graze, Dusty always hangs around for that last pat on the neck. He is the first one to come running the moment I arrive. He loves attention and wants to be in the middle of everything.

It was Dusty's rambunctious behavior—and not knowing anything about his under-saddle training except that he had been on the track—that caused my apprehension the day I decided to ride him. He had healed for more than a year now, and during our groundwork he had proven over and over how willing and intelligent he was. His knee had healed nicely—although he still walks with a limp when he has done too much cavorting. But we had the go-ahead from our vet to ride him at an easy walk.

As I stepped onto the mounting block the morning I decided to ride him, he didn't move except to turn and watch what I was doing. I let the reins slide through my fingers so he could have his head. I figured he had a right to participate in this, our first ride, anyway he saw fit, except by attempting to end the ride early by landing me on my behind. He kept his eye on me while I put my foot in the stirrup, and staring back at him, I smiled. Suddenly I knew we were going to be just fine.

I settled my weight in the saddle. Dusty looked calmly forward and stood quietly with one ear cocked back toward me. I gently put my legs on him and he moved off like a perfect gentleman. I was so proud of him and his incredible ability to trust. I'd never dreamed that he would come so far.

On that first ride, I think I got answers to those questions I kept asking myself the day he came to us and I sat leaning against his stall while he slept, thinking about good and evil. This is in defense of evil, I guess, but if you don't have bad, how do you measure good? And if Dusty's life hadn't gone exactly as it had, including all the horror and pain he had endured, I never would have ended up with him. I realized that if Dusty had been born to conscientious owners, he wouldn't have been run till his legs were destroyed as a two-year-old, and he wouldn't have been sent to an unscrupulous horse trader who starved and abused him. If I hadn't gone with my friend to look at her horse that day, and if they had taken Dusty to slaughter a few days sooner, I never would have seen him. Had another person seen the pain in his eyes and been moved to do something—if just one person in this chain of abuse had had any sense at all—that person would have realized what an amazing boy he is, and he would have never been mine. I felt as though everything in his life had led him to me, and more than anything, I was thankful—thankful that events happened the way they did and that Dusty was here with us and would never hurt again.

Dusty is nine years old now and we don't ride him anymore. In fact, we barely rode him past that period after he had healed. No one has the right to ask any living thing to give to the point of physical and emotional destruction, and Dusty gave more in the first two years of his life than any horse should give in a lifetime. He deserves to be allowed to simply be a horse.

He has some days when there is swelling in his knee, causing him mild but obvious pain. Periodically, we have discussed treatment options with our vet and have concluded that most of us have knees more painful and in worse shape than Dusty's. He has a pretty good life and is clearly very happy. He spends his days on a fifteen-acre pasture of lush grass with two other geldings and one very playful donkey.

He stands without a halter for grooming, and turns his head this way and that to watch everything I do. We rarely even have to put a halter on him, and we never tie him, yet he doesn't wander off and he stands for hours as I fuss over him. He devours apples, carrots, pretzels, and anything else he can get us to hand over. If we pat his neck enthusiastically and tell him what a good boy he is, he bobs his head up and down and makes a high-pitched nicker that makes everybody laugh. He loves to show off but acts crushed if I scold him for getting a little too full of himself. When we pull in the drive he runs along with the truck, bucking and kicking along the fence line as a welcome home.

He still steals hats off our heads, but now he runs away across the pasture so proudly, his head high in the air, a hat clenched in his teeth. I am constantly amazed by him. He is the most comical, rambunctious, wonderful horse, and I love him with all my heart. I can't imagine him not being a part of our lives.

Things seem to unfold as they should in life, and if it was evil that set Dusty before us, then so be it. The facility where I found Dusty has since been shut down. The woman running the place was indicted and convicted by the FBI for murdering horses for insurance money. ♘

Dusty, taking off with another stolen hat.

Annie

I COULD BARELY BELIEVE WHAT WAS HAPPENING. The little mare I named Annie had only been with us at Proud Spirit a little more than two weeks, and the entire time had been a fight for her life. Now it seemed like she was giving up. I had just witnessed her collapse in gut-twisting slow motion, and she was now lying on the floor of her stall struggling to breathe. I ran to her side and knelt down, lifting her head onto my lap. She quietly rested there as I smoothed her mane. Through my anguish and tears I looked into her tired eyes and told her how sorry I was that we couldn't do more. She stared up at me. The look on her face seemed to say that she had accepted this fate. It was almost as if she were comforting me, telling me everything would be all right. But it wasn't all right. I wanted her to live. I didn't want her to accept what was happening, I wanted her to fight.

But more than anything I wanted her to have the love she deserved. I wanted her to know that this sanctuary would be her home, these horses would be her herd mates, that pond would be her place to swim, and these people would care for her and feed her for the rest of her life. I just wanted to let her be a horse. She was only twelve years old. Had she ever felt a kind hand? Had she ever known any of these things?

I watched her sides heaving to get oxygen to her weakened lungs. I looked at her flared nostrils and rigid mouth and tried to smooth the furrows in her brow. And then once again I looked into her eyes. I'd never seen such weary eyes. They told me what I needed to do.

"I know, Annie . . . " I told her through my choked sobs. "I know, sweet girl." As I rubbed her neck and smoothed her mane, she was clearly telling me that enough was enough.

We had been entrusted to bring this precious mare some comfort. She had been brought into our lives by fate and we had been blessed with the opportunity to give her a loving home, to care for her to the very best of our ability and give her all the security we could provide. And we wanted her to have these things—we wanted her to have them more than anything in the world. But a mighty opponent had taken hold of Annie's health and proved itself stronger than everything we had to fight back with. She was getting worse by the hour. And so the trust that had been placed upon us to restore her health and make her a part of this family had gone full circle. Now she needed us to unselfishly help her cross over and join another family. She needed us to end her suffering and let her go to a better place, where she would never hurt again.

I leaned down and kissed Annie's cheek, her glorious soft brown eyes looking up at me, and I at once felt deeply blessed that she had come into our lives and shattered that we couldn't do more for her. I left her then, for just a moment, to make that phone call she needed me to make.

The only thing we knew about Annie was that she had been found by an organization that rescues dogs. It was located in a small town in the center of the state, about two hours from our ranch.

Diane, who runs the rescue, got an anonymous phone call about several abandoned dogs on a vacant piece of property out in the country. Several of her volunteers headed out immediately, armed with crates and leashes to retrieve the dogs and bring them into the shelter. They were startled to discover an emaciated horse standing in the scant shade of a dilapidated barn. The caller had not mentioned a horse. Diane phoned me and explained the situation as soon as her volunteers returned with the seven flea-infested, starving dogs.

"Mel, there's an emaciated horse on the property," she said. "Do you have room for her at Proud Spirit?" I told her we did.

Diane spent the next few days getting the mare secured into her custody. There was minimal red tape, as the animals were abandoned. Then she had her vet do a quick once-over on the mare and draw blood to make sure she didn't have anything contagious before I brought her home.

I made some phone calls to various friends to find one who might be able to make the two-hour drive to help me get the mare and bring her back to Proud Spirit within the next few days. I never could see the sense in spending the money to buy a trailer of our own when there were always so many other pressing needs for the horses in our care. And I've always been fortunate that I could rely on numerous friends when I needed to haul. And this time, my friend Ted was able to help.

Ted is a rough and tough old cowboy who spent his younger years riding bulls in the rodeo. His elbow had been broken, his shoulder dislocated twice, and his nose rearranged on his face several times. His faded jeans barely maintain a foothold on his lanky frame. His shaggy gray hair always hangs in errant wisps, which he is constantly pushing off his weathered face. This rough appearance belies the fact—and he isn't ashamed to admit—that he cried like a baby when his much-loved horse died of kidney failure after complications from a rattlesnake bite.

Diane was keeping the little mare with a friend who had a place on five acres. Her name was Pam and the horse had been at her house for about a week. Ted and I made the two-hour trek and easily found the address. When we pulled into the driveway, I noticed a barn at the back of the property with several horses dozing in the shade of an oak tree. I wondered which one we had come for. Just then a woman walked out of the house and lifted her hand in a friendly wave. Ted and I waved back as we pushed the truck doors closed and made our way to the gate.

"You must be Mel. Any trouble findin' me?" she asked.

"No, not at all. It's pretty over here," I told her as I looked out over the surrounding land. "I've never been in this part of the state."

I introduced Ted and turned my attention to the barn. "Which one is she?" I asked.

"Oh, she's not with them. She's way too weak to be with another horse and I didn't wanna take a chance of any of mine pickin' on her. I've only got the one pasture, so I had to put her up here in the yard." She turned slightly and tipped her head toward the house. "I guess she's made her way around to the other side. Grass is greener over the septic tank, ya know," Pam chuckled and Ted and I grinned at her little joke.

"I'll go get her if you're ready to head on back home." She started for the yard, then stopped and turned back to face us, her stare directed right at me. "She looks pretty bad. Just so ya know."

I stood there as she walked away, then stepped up to the gate and rested my cheek on my hands along the top rail. I was looking to the side, watching Pam's horses out by the barn. Suddenly I heard Ted behind me mutter under his breath, "I'll be damned." I turned to look at him, wondering what he was cussing about. Our eyes met, then he shifted his gaze over my shoulder to the spot where Pam had disappeared around the corner of her house a moment before. He nodded for me to turn around.

Pam was walking toward us, leading the mare up to the gate. "Aw, gees," I breathed out with despair as they neared and I saw the condition the horse was in. I opened the gate to allow Pam and the horse to come through. I felt my throat tighten as the horse slowly shuffled past me. She was horribly emaciated and covered in open sores. Her hipbones and spine were painfully apparent. Pam handed me the lead rope and stood back so I could get acquainted with the little horse. Ted set his calloused hand on the mare's neck, then went to ready the trailer, shaking his head as he went.

The day Diane called me about this mare she had described her physical condition, and just now Pam had warned me that she looked bad, but something like this never really seizes your consciousness until it's standing in front of you. And what stood before me now was simply the skeleton of a horse. I glanced back at Pam, and like Ted, I could only shake my head. I was actually worried about how the little mare would manage the two-hour ride home in the trailer.

"Did you name her yet, Pam?" I asked.

"No. I've just been calling her 'Li'l Girl.' Tell ya the truth, the way she looked when Diane first brought her out, I didn't think she'd still be alive by today. I was tryin' not to get too attached. The vet told me to feed her a bunch of real small meals several times a day and, believe it or not, she's put on a tiny bit of weight."

I reached up and rubbed the mare's forehead, and then hugged her head to my chest. It was simply heartbreaking to look at her. And I don't really know where the name came from, but while I was holding her I whispered in her ear that we would call her Annie, our little horse found on an abandoned piece of property in the middle of nowhere.

Annie ended up tolerating the ride in the trailer just fine. The first half hour of the drive home I kept jumping out of the truck at every stop sign and red light to check on her, but she actually seemed to have perked up and was looking around at her surroundings with renewed interest. I was able to relax for the remainder of the trip. When we pulled into our driveway at Proud Spirit, Annie was the first one to yell out a hello to the other horses. Naturally, they all came running to investigate the new arrival.

We put Annie in a small paddock by herself to let her settle in, and we planned to leave her there for at least a month. She could see the other horses and get to know them over the fence line, but she would need to regain her strength before she could be put in with the rest of the herd. I phoned our vet, Dr. Michael Brooks, and made an appointment for him to come out the following week and give Annie a thorough examination and update her vaccinations. The only immediate attention she needed was regular meals, so we were in no real rush for him to come out.

Aside from severe emaciation and those open sores, Annie also had foot problems and needed to be seen by our farrier to have her feet trimmed. I looked in her mouth and guessed she was under fifteen, and I could tell her teeth hadn't been tended to in years, if at all. I was concerned about her very shaggy coat and was sure she was full of parasites. The infestation was more than likely dangerously compromising her intestines in such a way that her system did not allow her to shed her thick winter coat, even in the middle of the hot Florida summer. We went ahead and wormed her, and a few days later that long heavy coat finally started to fall off. We were sad to discover that with all the extra hair gone, she looked even thinner than when she first arrived.

All these things, such as her weight and feet and teeth, would be addressed in good time. But until then, I spent those first few days just getting to know Annie—doctoring wounds, giving her treats, and grooming her coat. She was an incredibly sweet girl, and even though she appeared to have endured a lifetime of suffering and neglect, she seemed to love the attention we were giving her. I couldn't wait for the day when she had regained her health and could actually join the herd. I was so anxious for her to find a buddy. And what a joy it would be to see her running and acting her age.

One afternoon before the appointment with our vet I noticed that Annie seemed to be developing a slight respiratory problem, causing her mildly labored breathing. Dr. Brooks was due the following afternoon so we decided we would wait and see what his examination revealed.

⊍

"How long has she had this nasal discharge, Mel?" Dr. Brooks asked during his examination.

"It started late last night," I replied.

"She's got a slight fever, too . . . " he started to say.

"That's new. It was normal when I took her temperature before I went to bed," I interrupted.

He nodded. "Okay, I think we'll address her breathing difficulty before we do anything else. I don't want to overload her with treatment. I'm going to draw blood and run some tests. Then we'll talk about how to proceed."

In the days that followed we stayed in close contact with Dr. Brooks, but Annie seemed to be getting progressively worse. The medication he left to ease her breathing had helped for about forty-eight hours, but it wasn't working any longer. Annie was coughing, her fever had increased, and the nasal discharge was worse. Dr. Brooks returned and was disheartened to see that Annie's condition had indeed deteriorated.

We started her on a round of antibiotics and a different respiratory drug. I spent that evening gently hosing down Annie's legs and neck trying to reduce the fever. Around midnight I went to bed, but checked her several times through the night. She was stable, but clearly struggling.

The following morning Annie had lost interest in grazing and she wouldn't even look at her grain. This terrified me. Horses are always hungry, and from the moment we'd brought Annie home, she'd had a good appetite. For the first time in two weeks,

I felt like she was giving up and I just couldn't believe it. I'd known this recovery period was going to be an uphill climb for Annie, and I'd known her health was borderline at best. But I had truly believed we were going to get her well. She had sparkled with genuine interest at everything we did with her, and she'd simply glowed with the attention she was getting. I had seen the will to live in her eyes!

But now, even though her stall door was propped open and she had free access to her paddock, she just stood with her head hanging. I called Dr. Brooks again.

"Mel, I'm not going to give you false hope. She's got a lot going on and I'm not encouraged by how rapidly she seems to be declining. Hose her off periodically to keep her cool, and try to get the meds down her as best you can. Call me if there's a change."

I hung up the phone, then sat in the aisle way opposite Annie's stall, helplessly watching her struggle to breathe. I noticed her right leg started to tremble as she slowly tried to kneel down. But she was too weak to hold her own weight. I jumped up and ran to her side just as she collapsed.

Down on her side, she lay perfectly still. I crouched beside her and put my head near hers to see if she was breathing. She was, but the reality was that she was in serious trouble, and with a heavy heart I knew what she needed me to do. But before I did anything, I lifted her head onto my lap.

"I know, Annie . . . I know, sweet girl," I murmured through my tears. I told her I loved her and I thanked her for sharing her extraordinary spirit with us. I told her we were truly blessed that she had come into our lives, even for this very short time. And I told her how sorry I was that her time here on this earth had been filled with such pain.

I leaned down and kissed her on the cheek, then left to make the call I had been dreading.

Annie was euthanized that day, within a few hours of my call to Dr. Brooks. After letting her rest for a short time, with our help she was able to weakly get up on her feet once again. We slowly and quietly walked her out to a peaceful wooded area under an old oak tree. I tried to give her some treats, but she wouldn't eat. I let the chunks of apple fall from my hand. I took a moment to smooth her mane and tell her once again how much I loved her. Dr. Brooks gently asked me if I was ready to say good-bye. I looked up at him and met his kind eyes. He had been through so much with us over the years we'd been taking care of all these downtrodden horses. He'd seen me through some marvelous successes and so much heartache. I was deeply grateful for his compassion and genuine love for all animals. I smiled at him, my chin quivering and my cheeks smeared with tears. He reached out and squeezed my arm. "You're doing the right thing, Mel. And you've given her more love these two weeks than she's probably known her entire life."

"That's what makes this so hard, Mike. I wanted her to get well and have a lifetime of love with us." My voice trailed off and I told him I was ready.

Dr. Brooks lightly sedated Annie. While we waited for that to take effect, I held her head to my chest and cupped my hands over her eyes, whispering to her, "Go easy."

"Are you ready for me to give the final dose, Mel?" he asked gently.

Unable to talk, I shut my eyes and pulled Annie even closer, then nodded for him to go ahead. I was still hugging her as the life slipped from her weakened body.

Neither one of us spoke, and for just a moment I looked away from the little sorrel mare who had come so briefly into our lives. The June sky was a remarkable, brilliant blue. Towering white thunderheads were building to the east, promising to bring our regular Florida afternoon shower. The two hundred or so cattle that belonged to the ranch directly behind our property were making their daily journey to the large pond in the middle of the thousand acres. They headed to this spot at just about this same time every day to cool off and quench their thirst. The sound of the mamas bellowing to their calves to keep up and stay with the herd filled the air, familiar to me as the sound of the wind. To the west of our ranch, I could hear but could not see our neighbor mowing his pastures. There was something almost soothing about the chugging din of the tractor and the faint smell of freshly mown hay wafting across the fields.

Everything around me was normal—so much so that there was almost an air of complacency. The sights and sounds and smells filled my senses with the affirmation that everything was going along as it should . . . everything except for this little horse lying dead at my feet.

I found some wildflowers at the back fence line and kneeled down to place them along Annie's mane. I gently tucked her head and brought her legs into a sleeping foal position, smoothing her mane and forelock. She didn't even look like the same horse. She was at peace now, and her pain and struggling had ended. Her sides were still, not heaving to get air. Her mouth was no longer rigid and tight. The furrows in her brow were gone. The deep, painful lines around her eyes had eased.

As I knelt on the ground, Dr. Brooks gave my shoulder another squeeze. I looked up at him and weakly smiled a silent thank you as he left me to continue his round of scheduled appointments. I stayed on the ground beside Annie.

Several times I rearranged the flowers along her mane. I think I needed to keep trying to make things right. I still needed some control over this loss. Rearranging the flowers was all that was left for me to do.

Eventually, I smoothed her forelock one final time and ran my fingers through her silky mane. Then I leaned down and kissed her lifeless cheek. With my hands still resting on her shoulder, I sat back on my heels and lifted my face to the sky. To her freed spirit I said aloud, "Run, Annie . . . run as fast as you can, sweet girl. You'll never hurt again." ♘

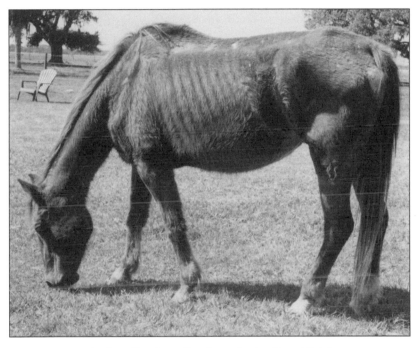

Annie, a few days after she arrived at Proud Spirit.

Storm Dancer

I HAD JUST GOTTEN HOME FROM WORK and hit the play button on the answering machine as I walked by on my way to the bedroom to change my clothes. From the hall I heard the recording, "Melanie, this is Allen at the Bar D. Someone contacted us about a horse that's in trouble. I was callin' to see if you could help. Give a call back as soon as you can and I'll fill you in."

I've known Allen for several years. He is the manager of one of the largest feed stores in this area, the Bar D. He's a real quiet man, but also one of the kindest, nicest people I have ever met. Allen knows all about Proud Spirit and keeps my number handy in case he hears about—as he said on his message—a horse that's in trouble. I picked up the phone and called him right then.

"Hey, Allen, it's Mel," I said when he came to the phone. "What's up about a horse in trouble?"

"Hi, Mel, thanks for callin' back. Listen, a woman called here yesterday. I don't even know who she is. Anyway, she asked us if we knew of anyone that could take in a horse that isn't being fed. It seems he belongs to an elderly lady who can't take care of him anymore and she's not feeding him. Some neighbors have gotten together, one of them the woman who called here, and they've been buying hay and throwing it over the fence for him, but I guess he looks pretty bad. They were gonna call animal control, then decided they didn't wanna cause trouble for the old woman. One of them went to talk to her about giving him up willingly if they could find him a home. I guess she said she would let him go. That's when the neighbor called here."

"Doesn't the woman who owns the horse have any family, Allen?"

"Yeah, I guess there's an adult grandson, but they said he doesn't come around too often and doesn't seem to care about the horse. The woman who called here said if the horse isn't out of there in less than a week they will call animal control. She said mainly because she didn't think he would live much longer than that and she didn't want a dead horse rotting in the weeds next door to her backyard."

"Nice," I said, not trying to hide the sarcasm in my voice.

"Yeah, no kiddin'. I really don't know much else. I have the elderly lady's phone number. Maybe you could go over there and see what the situation is. I'd sure hate to see animal abuse charges pressed against the old gal either 'cause of illness or a touch of senility."

I agreed with Allen and took down the number he had for the elderly woman. He said her name was Mrs. Percy. As soon as Allen and I hung up, I tried to reach her. Almost on the first ring, a woman with a very strong Southern accent picked up the phone.

But hers wasn't just any Southern accent. It was an accent indigenous to a strong and proud breed of people called Crackers. Their speech has a lilting cadence, unique unto itself, that makes it hard to define with the written word. Fiercely independent, the ancestral Cracker families chose the isolation that the interior of Florida provided. Some made their way raising cattle on the vast prairies or tending neat, orderly rows of orange groves that grew out of the lush and fertile hammocks. Still others fished the creeks and freshwater lakes for bass, blue gill, speckled perch, and bream. There were even those who hunted alligators and frogs from the endless swamps and marshes. They sold the bounty of their hard work in the larger towns to the north, such as Gainesville and Tallahassee. This was before air conditioning, condos, Disney, and highways that weren't more than a horse path at the time. They had a special and rare ability to see the glory of nature all around them and give thanks for the tiniest of blessings while enduring hardships that would bring lesser men or women to their knees. This ingrained trait, which defines the word grit, remains in the present-day descendants of the Crackers who tamed the harsh Florida wilderness.

"Yes, who's there?"

"Hello, is this Miz Percy?" I asked.

"Yes, who's this?"

"Miz Percy, my name is Melanie. I was told you may want to find a new home for your horse. I'm calling to see if I can be helpful in any way."

I was startled when Mrs. Percy began to weep softly and then stopped just as suddenly to exclaim with indignation, "Ever'body keep a'tellin' me I got to let him go. They say he not bein' fed. I tol' that gran'boy a'mine, he gots to feed Piney ever' day. I cain't get out there to do it m'self, ya see. Oh, Lo', what I gonna do without my Piney. He my boy, ya see. That gal down the road, she say somethin' got to be done, but I don' know what I can do. Piney, he a fine hoss. I don' rightly know what I would do without him."

"Miz Percy, would you let me come over and we can talk about it some, and then you can decide if maybe you think Piney might have a good home with me?"

"You likes hosses, does ya?" she asked. "He a fine hoss, my Piney is. I calls him my boy."

After we had talked a while longer, Mrs. Percy gave me her address and I headed out right away. I recognized the street name and headed in that direction, figuring I'd find her house once I got in the area. Suddenly it hit me—that street is in town! How can that be if the horse is on the property? I thought about calling her back but decided to continue. When I turned onto her road I realized that fifteen years earlier this part of town was out in the country. Now there were new houses all along this road, one identical to the last, all crammed together with no identity. Further on towards the end of the road the new houses stopped and there was a fairly large parcel of land with a modest, run-down older home almost completely hidden by a fence overgrown with brush. I checked the numbers on the mailbox—this was it.

Making my way to the door I had to step over broken lawn equipment, rain-soaked chunks of carpet, rusty bikes, car batteries, and an endless array of other trash. The grass was way past my ankles. Weeds had long ago taken over any landscaping around the house. There were several cars off to the side of the driveway, all in various stages of being dismantled. Doors, engine parts, wheels, and tires were everywhere.

"Miz Percy!" I called out as I knocked on the door.

"Jus' c'mon in," I heard her holler from inside. I was a little troubled that she would tell a stranger to just come on in, but I walked the few steps up a homemade plywood ramp and turned the doorknob.

The inside of the house was as dark as a cave. I had to stand for a moment with the door open to let my eyes adjust to the gloom.

"I'm in here. Jus' c'mon in," she said again. I closed the door and made my way down a short entrance hall. I have to admit that once I emerged into the living area and my eyes adjusted to the dark, I had forgotten I'd come here about a horse. Mrs. Percy sat bolstered by numerous pillows in an enormous lounge chair that practically swallowed her whole, a tattered quilt across her lap. She was tiny and frail. Some strands of her unkempt silver hair hung from a loose bun atop her head. She wore no glasses, and I was immediately struck by her eyes. There was something about them, something almost familiar.

Several dishes were lying about with moldy half-eaten meals on them. Everywhere I looked, on every surface, there were towering stacks of old magazines, newspapers, and mail. All the furniture was antique and of a heavy dark oak, too big for the room and crowding every corner. Adding to the oppressive feeling in the room, there were deep burgundy brocade curtains drawn across all the windows, blocking out any light—except for one window that looked out to the back of the property. A small lamp glowed from an ornate oak table beside where Mrs. Percy sat, the bulb's stark, white light washing over her and making her pale skin look almost translucent.

There was a metal walker sitting in front of the table to her left, and to her right sat a low footstool covered in the same brocade material as the dark curtains. I removed the stack of papers that buried the stool. We still had not spoken, and as I sat down on the stool, Mrs. Percy thrust her chin forward and squinted her eyes, peering directly at me.

"You Melody?" she asked in a firm voice.

"You can call me Mel," I said and smiled up at her from my little perch at her feet.

"You come here to talk to me about my boy, Piney?" she asked. She started to cry again. I didn't answer her, wondering how I should proceed. "What I gonna do without my boy, he my boy. Oh, Lo', what I gonna do," she continued.

After a moment, Mrs. Percy put her hand over her eyes and rested her head. She had stopped crying right away and almost seemed to doze now. I looked at the paper-thin skin of her hand and saw the blue veins, thinned with age, that carried her blood. She looked like she had been strong in her youth. There was an air about her that spoke of her being a remarkable woman. I put my hand gently on her knee to rouse her.

This reminded her of my presence and she looked up at me and smiled but did not speak. "Miz Percy," I quietly asked, "do you have someone who comes to help you?"

"Oh, yes, I got real sick a whiles back and spent some time in a hospital. Now I got one of them home nurses that come to the house. She come ever' day." She reached down and took my hand, which was still on her knee. Her skin felt cool and soft like velvet against my own, which was calloused and rough. She turned my hand over and ran her fingers along my palm.

"You been workin', gal," she chuckled and her eyes sparkled a little. Then she seemed very tired again and let her head drop back against the pillow behind her head.

"But what about meals and cleaning?" I asked.

"That gran'boy a'mine s'posed to come around. I reckon he don' do all he should. Things been bad since I lost my husband." She lifted her head, looked me right in the eye, and proudly said, "He built this house, ya know." Then she let her head fall back on the pillow, her gaze searching the walls of the home she had shared with her husband.

"We used to own all this property, all up and down this road and way on yonder to the south there. It was t'ward three-hundred acre, I think. I don't rightly remember now. Hoo boy! Me and Piney, we would ride all through the woods there." She chuckled again and smiled at the memory, her thoughts in the past as she looked right by me and seemed to forget once more that I was there. She was still holding my hand and I gently squeezed hers.

"Anyway, they used to be woods there. Now they all gone. Seem to me that ever'thing is gone now." She talked at length about her husband and the life they had made for themselves when this was still rural land. She told me of clearing a spot for the house from the stand of hardwoods, working side by side with her husband. She spoke of working in the blazing sun to put up a garden and surviving tremendous hurricanes before there were such things as radar and television to warn you of their coming. I was fascinated listening to her, but after more than an hour of Mrs. Percy intermittently talking and dozing, I realized that she needed to rest and I needed to be getting home.

"Where is Piney, Miz Percy?" I asked.

"He out back there, I reckon." She turned her head to the left and nodded at the window. "That's why I leaves them curtains open, so's I can see him when he come 'round for a treat. I cain't take him one no more, but the ol' boy, he sure 'nough still come around."

"When was the last time you saw him?" I asked.

"I reckon I sees him ever' day." She said this more to herself and turned her head again to look out the window. I followed her gaze. Her window looked out onto a screened-in porch. All the windows on this porch had been covered with a heavy plastic, but the plastic was so old it had clouded over and I realized that Mrs. Percy couldn't possibly see out this window when, or if, Piney came for his treats.

"Do you mind if I go say hi to Piney, Miz Percy?"

With her permission I walked outside and around to the back of the property. There was a sagging, rusty barbed-wire fence line not too far from the house. It came off an old rickety barn and looped around to the back, but the dense six-foot-high weeds in this pasture made it difficult to see where Piney might be. I went to the fence and called out, "Hey, buddy!" Immediately, from the back of the pasture there came a strong, almost playful, high-pitched whinny. I sort of laughed to myself and thought that he can't be in that bad of shape. He sounded more like a young and healthy two-year-old colt calling to a paddock full of willing mares than a severely neglected elderly gelding on his last legs.

As I stood waiting for him to emerge from this jungle of weeds, I called out again, just to encourage him along. And just as before, he answered with another enthusiastic response. Sometimes, people who aren't familiar with horses will see one that is elderly and wrongly assume that the horse isn't being cared for because of a swayed back, or a few ribs showing, or perhaps because the horse stands with his head hanging. Oftentimes the horse really is fine, he's just old, and these are all symptoms of old age in many horses. From the sound of his strong response, I started to think that maybe this was the case here.

Maybe the grandson was feeding him. Maybe everything was fine and Piney could stay with Mrs. Percy. Maybe the horse didn't look like the picture of health, but he really was just fine. If this was so, I would speak to the neighbors and reassure them that Mrs. Percy's horse was okay.

I could see the weeds swaying before I saw Piney, and when the weeds finally parted and he came up to the fence line, I certainly wasn't expecting what stood before me. Involuntarily, I covered my gaping mouth with my hand as I sharply took in my breath. He was terribly emaciated. He was a tall roan Appaloosa with great, big, beautiful dark eyes, but his coat was dull and lifeless, he was covered with flies, and he was just so, so thin. What was most startling, though, was his right hip. It jutted out in a deformed manner, and every joint in his right leg was frozen solid. He had a horrible time with forward motion, having to drag this stiff leg behind him. My heart ached at the sight of him.

The moment he saw me he came right to where I stood, nickering over and over, starving for grain, and starving for attention too, it seemed. I reached for his long neck and patted him gently, still shaking my head. After ridding myself of the initial shock, I walked around to a gate and into the barn to see if I could find some grain. The dirt floor of the barn and the stalls were lower than the surrounding land, and the recent rains had pooled there, making a filthy, muddy mess. The constant moisture, mixed with urine and manure, made it impossible to breathe. I quickly looked around for some feed. There was an open bag lying up on a work bench. I scooped a bit of it into my cupped hands to see if it was moldy. Surprisingly, it looked and smelled okay, so I grabbed a bucket, threw in several handfuls, and went back to where Piney waited. I held the bucket for him while he ate, and I told him all about Proud Spirit and that I would be bringing him home with me.

Shortly, I returned to the house and sat down once again on

the low stool next to Mrs. Percy. I smiled at her, but I didn't say anything. She did not speak either but looked into my eyes in such a way that told me she accepted my presence, as if she felt I was supposed to be there. Though we had only just met, it seemed that something spiritual had brought us together. Anyone could have come in here and rescued this horse, but there would not have been this connection. Something unseen comforted her as she smiled back at me. The corners of her mouth barely turned up, and her eyes did not waver from mine. She understood.

Mrs. Percy and I still did not speak as I picked up the phone that was on the small table beside her chair to call my friend and neighbor, Carla. I wanted to see if there was any way she could meet me with her trailer and get Piney out of there today. Carla was home and anxious to help, but she had previous commitments, so we decided it would have to wait till the next day.

When I had set the phone back down, I took a deep breath and scooted my stool closer to Mrs. Percy's knees. She could have easily heard me on the phone just then, but she had laid her head back on the pillow and closed her eyes, so I had no idea if she was aware of what I'd just asked Carla. I was heartsick for her, sitting here alone day after day, and I wondered what she felt as she looked back on her life. She and her husband had obviously worked hard, acquired land, built a home, raised a family. And now here she sat, as alone and neglected as her beloved Piney.

"Miz Percy . . ." I set my hand on her knee. She opened her eyes and turned to look at me. "Miz Percy, Piney is not being fed. There was no water in his trough and he is drinking from rain puddles. I'm afraid that he will die if we leave him here. I would like you to tell me that Piney can come home with me. If you let him come home with me I'll make you a solemn promise that he will be loved and cared for the way you want him to be cared for. The way he deserves to be cared for."

There were tears welling in her eyes, and she looked away from me and out toward the plastic-covered windows. Her voice was barely a whisper, "He my boy. What I gonna do without my boy?" I took her hand in mine and quietly said again, "Miz Percy, Piney is not being fed. He needs to be taken care of."

"I'm eighty-two year old, ya know. I've had Piney for nigh on fifteen years. I rode him right on up till the rascal got outen the fence and was hit by a car. Broke his hip, ya know. But he healed right up and seem to git along just fine. Couldn't ride him no more, but that was no matter. Ever' body kept a'tellin' me then I ought'a have him put to sleep, put him outen his misery, they say, but they don' know my Piney. He got a will to live, and he got more heart and spirit than most men I know."

"How old is Piney now?" I quietly asked.

"Oh, I reckon he t'ward twenty year old now, or more. I don' rightly remember. You say he not bein' fed?" I shook my head in response, and told her that he was terribly thin. She looked down at her hands and slowly shook her head.

"I tol' that gran'boy a'mine . . ." Her voice trailed off and she looked up at me again. There were tears in her eyes once more. "I reckon I'd be obliged iffen you do right by Piney. He surely done right by me." She put her hands over her face and started to weep.

I felt so helpless as I sat there, my own eyes filling with tears. She seemed to me like a beautiful deciduous leaf on a hardy oak—strong and resilient in the green of her youth, then even more glorious in the autumn of her life, fragile with the brilliant color of age. Now she was falling back to the earth to be covered over with the snows of winter and forgotten. I put my head down and let her cry. I have no idea how long we sat like that.

The next day Carla and I pulled up in her truck with her trailer in tow. There was a car in the drive that I hadn't seen the day before. I went up to the door while Carla waited outside. When I knocked, a neatly dressed woman opened the door, and before either of us could say a word I heard Mrs. Percy from the living room, "Who is it, Ellen?" Ellen smiled in a very friendly way but looked at me as if to say, " Well, you heard her, who are you?" I told Ellen who I was, then said, loudly enough for Mrs. Percy to hear, "It's Mel, Miz Percy. I've come for Piney."

"Well, jus' c'mon in!" she called.

Ellen and I made our way through the gloomy hall and sat down in the living room, me taking my spot on the low stool at Mrs. Percy's feet. I learned that Ellen was the nurse who came daily.

"I'm happy to see you here," I said to Ellen. "I was sorta worried about Miz Percy being here alone and all . . ." My voiced trailed off as I glanced in the older woman's direction and smiled.

Mrs. Percy waved off my concern saying, "Oh, I git along jus' fine. All this fuss, I swear."

"Well, you and I have different opinions about getting along just fine, don't we?" Ellen replied.

"Humph," Mrs. Percy muttered as she turned her face away from us. But her response was almost playful, and it was clear she and Ellen had a close relationship.

Ellen knelt down, placed a gentle hand on Mrs. Percy's knee, and said, "Her doctor and I have been working very hard on convincing her that she needs to go into a retirement home. She'll be able to meet new friends and get help with meals and bathing. In fact, I was happy to hear from Mrs. Percy just this morning that you're going to be taking her horse. This has been her biggest objection to leaving her home. Maybe now we can move this idea along."

Ellen stood to leave. She had already finished with her duties before I'd arrived. I was pleased she'd taken a moment to speak to me about Mrs. Percy's future. I thanked her, and we said good-bye. As Ellen quietly shut the door behind her, Mrs. Percy asked me if I was there to talk to her about Piney. "I'm here to bring Piney to my house, Miz Percy."

"You gonna do that today, huh?" She looked down at her hands for just a moment, then back at me. "Well, I reckon iffen this is the way things is gonna be, then it's the way they gonna be. You might as well take the things what belong to him. You go on out to that barn there and gits his blanket, and brushes, and whatever else you thinks he might need."

I smiled at the way she had rallied her emotional strength. She seemed very settled with the whole idea of Piney coming to live with me, almost relieved. I was given a glimpse of her strong personality and the way she must have taken charge when she was young and saw a need for some firm direction. I told her I would go on out and get things ready, and that before we left I would come back in and say good-bye to her.

I stood to go outside when Mrs. Percy stopped me. "I'm jus' wonderin' . . . will you bring Piney up to the door here so's I might say g'bye to him? I reckon I can get up to the door, huh?"

"Yes, ma'am, I believe you can. And if you can't, well, I'll bring Piney right on in the house and up to your chair." She chuckled at my foolishness about bringing a horse in the house and waved me away, still laughing. I was elated that she seemed so much better than the day before. She hadn't wept once about Piney leaving and I so badly wanted her to feel good about it. I couldn't bear the thought of her suffering.

Carla and I stowed in the bed of her truck the few things we found in the barn that looked like they belonged to Piney, and while she readied the trailer I went to halter him. I was going to have Carla hold him while I went back in the house and helped Mrs. Percy come say good-bye at the door. But I looked up and there she was! She stood with her walker in front of her and she leaned on it heavily, but there she was, smiling.

Suddenly, a beat-up, old-model sports car with a roaring muffler pulled into the driveway. I caught Carla's eye and looked at her like this might be trouble. I was guessing this was Mrs. Percy's grandson.

"What's goin' on here?" he thundered as he flung open the car door. He appeared barely out of his teens but was already over six feet tall. The stained, faded T-shirt he wore was several sizes too small and barely covered his fleshy stomach and exposed, pudgy arms, which looked as though they never saw the sun.

"You min' your own business, boy. I tol' you Piney gots to be fed and you not doin' it, when you knows I cain't do it m'self." Mrs. Percy said from the doorway. Her voice was shrill and she sounded nervous, as if she was scared to be talking this way to her grandson yet saw no other choice but to defy him and save her beloved Piney.

He turned and jabbed a pointed finger in her direction, "You git in the house!"

I glanced back at Carla, both of us incredulous that he would speak to his grandmother this way. As I stood holding Piney, the young man strode past me and went toward the barn, saying that he saw us in there from the road and wanted to know what we had taken. I angrily told him to go look in the bed of Carla's truck, that we only took what belonged with Piney. While he was in the barn, apparently checking to make sure we hadn't stolen anything, I walked Piney up to the door and to Mrs. Percy, who was waiting there. As we approached, she was able to see how thin he was. Her frail hand fluttered to her mouth. "Oh, Lo', never in all my days," she said, turning her head sharply away, as if she couldn't bear to look at him. She started to weep. I touched her arm, nudging Piney closer.

"Piney's going to be just fine, Miz Percy. He just needs a little weight on and he'll be fine. Go ahead and tell him good-bye. He knows you love him."

She put her forehead against Piney's neck, one frail hand reaching up to touch him and encircle him with her arm. He turned his head to her gently, clearly happy to see his old friend. Mrs. Percy closed her eyes and quietly told him something only he could hear. Then she turned from the old Appaloosa, crying softly, and went back into the house. There was a lump in my throat as I silently cursed the grandson for allowing this to happen to the only thing that gave her joy.

Carla had opened the door to the trailer and was standing inside. I walked Piney over and handed her the lead rope. We could hear thunder in the distance and looked up at the same time to scan the darkening sky. Just then the grandson came over and stood with his toes practically touching my own.

"Who said you could take this horse?" he demanded.

I backed up and scowled at him, "Who do you think said we could take him? Your grandmother did!"

"And how much did you pay her?" he asked angrily. My eyes widened in disbelief and I just stared at him for a moment, dumbfounded.

"I'll tell you what, son, your grandmother gave me this horse, and to avoid animal abuse charges being pressed against you, I suggest you simmer down," I calmly told him.

I knew it was foolish to goad him on or make him more confrontational. But when he threw his arm over Piney's back in a possessive and cocky manner, I saw red. He actually started to poke Piney in the ribs with his fingers in a very rough way.

"This is a good horse. Ya oughta have ta pay something for him," he was saying. Piney was jigging sideways, tossing his head, and with each poke to the ribs the poor horse sharply let out his breath.

"Stop poking him!" I yelled. "If you think he's such a good horse, why aren't you feeding him? This horse is near death and you are to blame! Why aren't you feeding him?"

He didn't answer me, nor did he stop jabbing Piney. Then it started to rain. My head was in a flurry as he continued to go on about what he thought we "were getting away with." I couldn't even listen to him as I tried to think of how we could get Piney loaded and away from this abusive life.

We didn't even know if Piney would load, or could load, with his injured hip and stiff leg. The rain was making matters worse—there were no mats in Carla's stock trailer and the metal floor was getting wet. I didn't see how Piney could possibly manage that step up onto a wet floor, especially now that Mrs. Percy's grandson had gotten him all agitated and upset. I knew one thing for certain, though. I wasn't leaving without this horse.

Then I felt Carla touch my shoulder. When I turned to look

up at her in the trailer, she handed me Piney's lead rope.

Carla is a study of contrasts. She looks delicate—one of the most feminine, prettiest women I know. I've never seen a man walk by her who didn't turn his head. She's also one of the most independent and able women I know. She was raised in the country and grew up working hard and learning to be strong. She could ride a horse practically before she could walk. She can rope a calf, shoot a gun, and throw hay better than most men. And if she's crossed in a threatening way she can be mean as a stepped-on rattler.

I saw her pick up a short length of chain that was lying on the floor of her trailer. She held both ends of the chain in one hand, and then let one end drop and hit the side of the metal wall of the trailer. She folded the chain in half again and let one end drop from her hand once more. Carla had adopted a casual stance, almost like she was just fussing with the chain, but each time it hit the metal wall it was clear she meant business. My courage was renewed with Carla's backup. I stepped closer to the grandson. The top of my head came about up to his chest, but I looked him in the eye and hissed through gritted teeth, "You should be ashamed of yourself for the way this horse looks, and you should be even *more* ashamed of the way you treat your grandma. *Now get your hands off of my horse!*"

He didn't move a muscle and stared right back at me. My heart was pounding, but my eyes never moved from his. Then, still keeping his eyes on mine, he slowly let his arm slide off Piney's back. He took a few steps backward, then turned and walked toward the house.

When he was out of sight I turned and looked at Carla, and only then did I let the air out of my lungs. She muttered, "Stupid son of a bitch." She dropped the chain back to the floor. Then looking at Piney, she said, "Let's get him loaded."

Carla took the lead rope from my hands and coaxed Piney forward. The thunder and lightning were moving in now, and it was raining even harder. I couldn't stop the negative thoughts in my head and feared that Piney would never load. He stepped up to the edge of the trailer, sniffed the wet floor, and backed away. I moved off so as not to crowd him, and Carla stepped deeper into the trailer for the same reason. We let him relax for a moment, and we all took a deep breath. The scene with the grandson had been distressing, and I knew that Piney was nervous. After a few minutes I calmly moved towards Piney's hindquarters as Carla coaxed him forward again with a gentle pressure on the lead rope.

All around us the thunder and lightning continued to crash and I silently prayed for Piney to have the strength and the courage to manage this step we so badly needed him to take. He responded to Carla's urging and moved up till his legs were against the back of the trailer. Once again, he bent down to sniff the metal floor. Then suddenly, just like a jackrabbit, he jumped right in, both back legs at once, and easily found his footing on the wet trailer floor! I couldn't believe how easy he made it look! Carla laughed at his agility in spite of that hip and stiff leg and said, "You want out of here, don't ya, boy!"

After we had gone a ways down the road Carla looked over to me and said, "Well, what are ya gonna name him, Mel?" Anytime I felt that a horse coming to Proud Spirit needed a new beginning, I always changed his name. Carla knew this.

I looked out the windshield at the rain coming down in sheets now and heard the distant thunder, and I thought about how this incredible horse had leaped into the trailer with the grace of a dancer. I nodded at my decision and said, "Storm Dancer." ♘

*After years of isolation, Dancer was thrilled to be with another horse and
was often seen licking Hank's coat.*

Maddy

DANCER WAS SETTLING INTO HIS NEW LIFE AT PROUD SPIRIT with amazing ease. He loved all the attention we were giving him, and every morning the very first thing he did was let out that high-pitched whinny of his to say hello, making sure we noticed him. We slowly put about one hundred and fifty pounds on him, careful not to let him get too heavy as he had a lot to contend with because of that broken hip. We were very conscious of the blessings that brought Dancer to our sanctuary and felt honored that we were able to provide him with the simple components of life that all horses need to be happy.

When we first brought Dancer home from Mrs. Percy's, a woman named Marla, who had heard that "Piney" was now living at Proud Spirit, contacted me and asked if she could come out to see him. The afternoon Marla arrived—many years ago now— turned out to be very emotional for the older woman. She told me she had owned Piney from the time he was weaned till he was about four years old, and she actually brought his baby pictures to show me. She had sold him when he was around four, and over the years she had tried to keep track of the tall Appaloosa's whereabouts. Marla knew that he was eventually bought by Mrs. Percy, and had just recently heard that she wasn't doing well, and as a result, Piney's health had been suffering. But at the time, Marla wasn't aware that things had gotten as bad as they had, or she surely would have intervened on behalf of this gentle horse she had known practically since his birth.

Marla and Mrs. Percy had several mutual friends. Marla told us that Dancer had not been with or even seen another horse in probably ten years. I simply cannot imagine how hard this must have been on him emotionally. Of all animals on earth, I think it is especially difficult for horses not to have a same-species companion for even a very short period of time, but for ten years! I believe this isolation is damaging to their very spirit. But, despite his lonely past, Dancer certainly displayed his excitement over seeing the other horses from the very first day we brought him home.

When he had recovered enough to function in a herd situation, we placed Dancer in one of the smaller pastures with a group of elderly geldings. Upon being turned out with his new buddies, Dancer immediately made friends with Hank, a very gentle, easygoing older Quarter Horse who came to us four years ago to retire because he was getting arthritic and was no longer rideable. Everything seemed to be going perfectly, but we continued to carefully monitor Dancer's introduction into the herd. For even though he could get around quite well, he still couldn't move as fast as the others with his injured hip and stiff leg, and we didn't want to take any chances on Dancer getting hurt.

Shortly after Dancer and Hank had been introduced, we were surprised to discover Dancer licking Hank's coat one afternoon, actually grooming him like a cat. Although horses do groom one another and scratch each other with their teeth, we had never seen this particular behavior in any of our horses before. We assumed it was the salty sweat Dancer liked. Regardless of how odd we thought it was, Hank appeared to be unfazed by Dancer licking him over and over. He just continued to graze, oblivious to the tall skinny Appaloosa following his every move. And Dancer, content as he could be with his new pal, thrived in this relationship. We were thrilled for him.

I was often reminded of Mrs. Percy's description of her beloved Piney and his noble character. We didn't know it at the time, but a heartbreaking situation would arise several years later during which he would prove to us just how noble he was. Just as she told me that day when we first met, he did indeed have a tremendous amount of heart and spirit.

Soon after his arrival, there emerged an indefinable gleam in his eyes, and we were never sure if it meant he was feeling mischievous or if it was simply contented happiness in the purest sense as he frolicked around like a young colt. For a horse who had suffered such hardships, both physical and emotional, he had overcome in a surprising way and exuded a genuine, infectious joy for life. His eyes genuinely sparkled.

We were continually astounded at how well Dancer managed to move about despite that stiffened leg and misshapen hip. We frequently witnessed him running across the pasture in his little jack rabbit gait, both back legs working as one. And we actually saw him bucking, as much as he could, when he became worked up with the rest of the herd.

I used to telephone Mrs. Percy once a week or so after I'd brought Dancer home to Proud Spirit. She was always thrilled to receive my calls and loved hearing about how her boy was doing. Sometimes she would cry as we talked about her horse, and she would express how she wished things could be different. About three months after she'd allowed us to take this very special horse from her side, Mrs. Percy died. I prayed that in her final days she was content knowing that her boy was loved and being cared for as she wanted him to be.

Dancer was our most recent addition to Proud Spirit, but in just a few weeks it seemed as though he had been with us forever. He was part of our family now, and during this tranquil time, the days and weeks passed with an easy familiarity, the contours of life uneventful at the sanctuary. All the horses were happy and healthy. The hard summer rains and blistering heat were beginning to subside with the approaching cooler weather of fall, making our daily routine less daunting. The horses too were feeling more energetic, and there was a lightness in the air as the oppressive humidity abated.

This particular day, I was just finishing up taking care of the horses. They were all fed, groomed, and turned back out to their respective pastures. I was sweeping out the barn when the phone in the tack room rang.

"Mel?" the voice on the other end sounded upset.

"What's wrong, Lisa?" I quickly asked.

Lisa is one of my closest friends. We are the yin and yang of best pals, for our personalities couldn't be more different. Lisa is quiet and introspective. She has a limitless depth for contemplating life and nature. There is a gentleness and serenity that seems to surround her, always, no matter what turmoil presents itself in her life. When she speaks, a calm purpose possesses her every movement and her hands are still. In contrast, if my hands were tied to my side, I wouldn't be able to talk. I generally have trouble sitting still, and when we are at a get-together with a group of friends, Lisa is the one who stands at the fringe, quietly listening, and I am the one in the center of the room telling ribald jokes. Yet somehow, in spite of our differences, or maybe because of them, we have become kindred spirits.

"Those people down the road from me are sending their horse off to slaughter!" Lisa exclaimed when I asked her what was wrong.

"What people?" I asked.

"I told you about them a few weeks ago. They're the people who have that mare with real bad arthritis and they're still riding her. The poor thing can barely walk."

I remembered now. Lisa had seen the horse being ridden by this family's children and she had told me about it one evening when we were talking on the phone. The mare limped when no one was on her back, and it was worse when the kids rode her, kicking her and pushing her to give more than the little horse was able to.

"What do you want me to do?" I asked. But I already knew what she wanted me to do. Lisa is fairly shy and not very comfortable approaching strangers. If this should escalate into a confrontational situation, it would be Lisa's nature to back down.

"We need to get her out of there," she said. "Euthanizing the horse if she's in a lot of pain is one thing. But to send her off to slaughter! She'll never survive that trailer ride, Mel. You need to go talk to them."

I readily agreed. After getting the address and all the particulars I could pull out of Lisa, we hung up. I put the broom away and decided to just go take care of this right away.

I pulled up in front of the house where Lisa said the horse was and parked on the street. Several loose dogs ran to the fence line, barking at me as I walked to the gate. I remained where I was, safely on the outside of the fence, and waited for someone to notice me. Soon a woman wearing a faded denim dress emerged from around the back of a small two-story house.

"The dogs don't bite!" she yelled as she waved for me to come on in. She had a friendly smile as I came through the gate. "What can I do for you?"

I noticed four small dirt paddocks off to my left. Each one contained a horse. There were no trees in the area where the horses were being kept, but each little paddock had a lean-to of sorts for shade. The fencing was a mixture of barbed wire, broken wood boards, bent gates, and ropes tying gaps together here and there. I couldn't tell which horse might be the one Lisa was concerned about, for they all looked elderly, depressed, and bored.

"I was told by a friend of one of your neighbors that you may have an elderly horse you're trying to get rid of." I said, trying to cover any trail that might lead to Lisa in case this got nasty.

"Yeah, we are. Our old mare, Candy." She turned to look behind her and pointed to the furthest paddock. "That's her at the end there. She's just no fun for the kids to ride anymore. Her legs are wooden . . . they're just wooden," she repeated, shaking her head. "She doesn't bend them at all and it jerks the kids around." She said this with a disgusted look on her face, as if it was something the mare was doing on purpose to make her children's lives miserable. I managed to keep my mouth shut as I nodded sympathetically.

"I've been looking for an elderly horse to be a companion to a horse I have now," I said. "She wouldn't be ridden anymore. I just need a pal for another horse. Would you be interested in letting me take her off your hands?" I refrained from mentioning our sanctuary. I didn't want her to think I was there in some imagined official capacity and get defensive.

"Sure, you could take her if you want, I guess." That was easy, I thought, smiling to myself. Until she continued, "You're in luck too. I put in a call to Bob Haines to come and get her. I don't really know him, but I guess he's some guy that buys old horses and takes them to slaughter."

"I know who he is," I interrupted.

"Oh, well, he already come out to look at Candy and said he'd give us eight hundred dollars for her. He told us he'd be back in a few days to get her, but we haven't seen him. And he never gave us any money, so if you want her, I guess my husband would say eight hundred dollars from you is just as good as from Bob Haines." My heart sank.

"Oh . . . geez . . . I really don't have that kind of money. I just thought if you wanted to find her a good home where she could retire and be taken care of, maybe it would be worth it to you to let me just have her," I said.

"Well, we can't do that. My husband would never agree to it. We need to get something out of her. We've had this horse a long time and we've spent a lot of money feeding her and things like that all these years. We need to get something back out of her."

I was dumbstruck. Get something back for feeding her all these years! It was beyond my comprehension that she couldn't hear the total stupidity of her own words. "What about all that the horse has done for you!" I wanted to yell. I was shaking with anger as I thought about so many horses imprisoned with owners of this mentality who don't feel that a horse who has safely taught their children to ride has given enough.

Our horses endure so much from us. We tirelessly devote ourselves to having the glossiest, best-behaved horse in the show ring. In this genre, it is paramount, and a source of pride, to be clever with a pair of clippers and a hundred dollars' worth of grooming supplies. But all too often we don't bother to educate ourselves about our horses' emotional health. We try to shove several thousand years of nomadic, grazing herd instinct into a twelve-by-twelve box stall, isolating horses from the touch and interaction with other horses that they so desperately need. We alter them physically, emotionally, and spiritually, take away everything that is natural and instinctual, all while relentlessly bending and pushing them to conform to our selfish idea of how they should live. Frequently, the sad result is that we end up causing and creating unwanted behavior, and then we do even more obnoxious things to them to stop the vices that we ourselves created!

Yet somehow, they stoically give and give, till they can give no more, and in return, we sell them, trade them, or send them off to slaughter trying to get the last dollar. We do everything except provide them with a deserved and dignified retirement or humanely help them, when the time comes, to cross over peacefully to a place where they will no longer hurt.

"I'll have to go home and talk to my husband," I told her, somehow managing to control the fury in my voice. And then I added, "I would really like to let this horse retire at our house. Would you think about taking less money and I'll get back with you tomorrow?"

She told me she would think about it, but she doubted they could accept less money for the horse they called Candy. I knew what Jim would do if I came home and explained the situation and told him what it would cost to save this poor little mare from the horrific ride to slaughter. Without even blinking, he would hand me the checkbook and tell me to go get her.

I walked out to my truck and tried to compose myself. I sat for a moment, when it suddenly struck me to attempt a different approach. I saw that the woman was still outside and I walked back to her gate. She noticed me and headed back my way to see what I wanted.

"I was just wondering, are you familiar with how Bob Haines transports these horses to slaughter?" I asked, trying to maintain a friendly tone of voice. As I was sitting in my truck it had dawned on me that maybe she was ignorant of the whole process. I was going to try to appeal to her sense of decency.

"What do you mean?" she asked.

"Well, do you understand what a nightmare it is for these horses to be transported to slaughter?" I asked

"I'm sure it's not the most pleasant thing for them, but death is a fact of life," she said.

"I'm not talking about death. I'm talking about you being able to control how this death occurs for a faithful companion who has given her best to your family for years and years," I said.

"You talk like she's a dog. . . . She's not a dog, ya know," she said, almost laughing.

"No, she's not a dog. But she is a living, breathing, feeling companion to this family. Whether you think of her that way or not, the fact remains. And when Bob Haines comes to pick her up you should know what will be on your hands if you allow him to take her," I said.

"What do you mean?" she asked again.

"Well, he will load her onto a thirty-five-foot stock trailer. He'll start heading north to the Florida border, stopping here and there to pick up other horses from other contacts. Then he'll head west for Texas, zigzagging all across the southern United States until that trailer is so full the horses can't move. The ones he picks up in Louisiana are lucky. They might be in the trailer for only a day or two at the most. But your little mare won't be so lucky. She'll have gone four or five days without food or water while Haines gets his hands on every unwanted horse he can find. If she falls down because she's lost her footing in all the urine and manure, she'll stay down. Most likely to get trampled by the others and killed." I said all this calmly, keeping my emotions in check. The woman's expression had changed from one of amusement to one of disbelief, which is what I had hoped for.

"That can't be legal. How can he get away with that?" she asked.

"It's not legal. Transporting horses to be rendered is regulated and it is supposed to be done humanely. But Bob Haines is a man of questionable ethics and I know for a fact that this is the way he operates. I also know that he repeatedly gets away with this. What happens en route to the slaughterhouse is not monitored. He lies about where the horses are coming from and how long they've been in the trailer, and he makes this run to Texas four to six times a year," I replied.

"My God! I had no idea," she said.

"I am willing to take the mare off your hands. If she needs to be put down, I will pay for her to be euthanized by my veterinarian in a kind manner. If she simply needs to be allowed to retire, I'll keep her at my place and take care of her for the rest of her life. But, please, don't send her off with Bob Haines. She'll never survive that ride with her arthritis. Let me know the absolute least amount of money you'll take for her and I'll pay you. I'll pay you tomorrow in cash if you let me have her," I pleaded.

We talked awhile longer and the woman said she would speak to her husband. Then she asked me why I would do this.

"I just like horses," I said, and left it at that. Even though she had been shocked by the things I told her about the trip to the slaughterhouse, I could tell that she would never understand the deeper meaning of why I do this. I could tell by the general poor condition of her horses and dogs, and I could tell by her callous response about needing "to get something back out of her" for feeding the horse all these years that she would never understand.

The next morning I phoned the woman's house to find out what she and her husband had decided. I planned to go directly to the bank as soon as we hung up and withdraw whatever amount of money they said they wanted for the little mare. I had spoken to my friend Carla the night before, and she was going to meet me with her trailer at the house where Candy lived as soon as I returned from town with the money. The nagging fear that Bob Haines would come for the mare between the time that I was at the woman's house the day before and this morning would not go away.

When I phoned the woman who owned Candy, I was astonished when she told me that I could have the mare for nothing. I never expected this, not in a million years, and I was elated—elated that these people would do the right thing, elated that I didn't have to take money out of the bank, but most of all I was elated for this little sorrel mare and the opportunity for her to know some peace. I called Carla, told her the good news, and since I didn't have to go into town, we headed out together to bring the horse home.

We loaded Candy without incident, but I was acutely aware—although not surprised—that no one in the family even said good-bye to her. When we arrived back home to Proud Spirit, Carla was unable to stay around and watch the mare settle in. She needed to get home and so we unloaded the horse in the yard and Carla went on her way. I renamed Candy "Madeline" . . . Maddy for short.

Maddy had a swayback from old age, and she was a bit on the thin side, although not too badly. Her feet were severely overgrown, causing her pain with every step, and they needed to be trimmed. I would get our farrier out as soon as possible, and after he tended to her we would decide how much of her limp was caused by arthritis and how much from just neglect. The only other problem was her coat. It appeared as though she hadn't received much grooming and as a result she had developed a fungal infection referred to as rain rot. This is easily remedied with some daily attention, and we would begin right away. All in all, aside from general neglect, she was in fair shape and in decent health for her age, which was around twenty-five or so.

I placed Maddy alone in the paddock near the barn, just as we always did with any new horse, giving her some time to familiarize herself with the strange surroundings. While she calmly sniffed around and munched on some grass, I leaned on the wood fence that comes off our barn and watched her from the yard. I felt very relaxed and content, and so thankful that things had gone the way they did.

As I was reflecting on how very quiet and serene it was, I suddenly realized that it shouldn't have been quiet and serene. None of the other horses had made much of a fuss over the new arrival, which wasn't normal. I looked out over our pastures and saw all of them peacefully grazing. There was no pounding of hooves coming to check out this most recent arrival. There was no posturing and straining at the fence line for a better look. Maybe they were getting too used to this kind of event. Or perhaps it was where Carla dropped us off; she didn't pull in past the barn as usual, but instead turned around by the house because she was in a hurry.

Or maybe there was another reason. A reason beyond any simple explanation of why things happen the way they do. For if the eighteen other horses we had at that time had created the usual confusion and noise, yelling and running to the fence line, what was about to happen may have been lost in the ruckus. And it was something I'll never forget for the rest of my life.

In all these years that we have been taking in abused, neglected, and unwanted horses, I have become used to witnessing some profound moments. I have not, however, become immune to their power. If anything, I am moved even more as I gain a better understanding of horses, their wants and needs, the fundamentals that motivate them, and all that they endure from us. I have been saddened for other horse lovers who have never witnessed what I have witnessed. Some incidents have sent me into fits of laughter; others have moved me to tears.

As I leaned on the fence, pondering the quiet, I noticed that Maddy had turned her attention to the adjacent pasture where Dancer now resided with an intense interest. Her ears were pricked forward and she had drawn her body up to its full height. I saw the slight weave of her head as she tried to focus on something there. Perplexed by this intensity, I followed her stare. She seemed to be looking directly at Dancer and Hank, who stood with their backs to Maddy, unaware of her scrutiny or even her presence, as they quietly ambled along and grazed.

Maddy took a few cautious steps forward, her head bobbing up and down in tentative excitement. I was still standing at the fence with my foot resting on the bottom rail, my chin resting on my hands along the top. I too drew myself up.

Something was happening, and the air was charged with anticipation. I walked through the gate to come closer, fascinated by what was taking place but careful not to interfere. Maddy's body language was unmistakable—she recognized one of these horses. Her eyes were bright and alert, and her nostrils flared as she took in several deep breaths of air searching for a familiar smell. Still unsure if the horse who was fixed in her sight was the one she knew, she took a few more steps. And then there was no doubt. She was sure. Her excitement was uncontained and she called out a heart-wrenching cry to this companion from her past!

Hank raised his head a few feet off the ground and glanced in Maddy's direction. Unconcerned, he plunged his nose back down into the ankle-high grass. At that very same moment Dancer's head shot straight up to the sky. He was still standing with his back to Maddy and did not turn around. He appeared frozen in place as he tried to grasp what was happening and absorb the sound of the voice he'd just heard. Impatient now, Maddy called again, and in her awkward wooden trot, she ran to the fence line, her eyes trained on Dancer. Freed from his shock by Maddy's insistent call, Dancer answered her as he simultaneously spun around. The instant he glimpsed her he tossed his head from side to side like a playful young colt. In his equally awkward trot, Dancer ran to meet Maddy at the fence!

I was the one who was now frozen in place. My eyes were wide and I dropped my hands to my sides, shocked by what was happening. They knew each other! I had never seen anything like this in my life. There was no doubt in my mind that they knew each other. But what was their history? Where had they been together? How long had it been since they had seen each other? What twists and turns of fate had put them together, however many years ago, so they could form this amazing bond, only to be pulled apart? And then years later, this very same fate would work in some elusive, magical way to bring them together once again. It had to have been at least ten years; we'd been told Dancer hadn't been with another horse in that long. It was incredible.

Maddy and Dancer now stood at the fence line, their noses pressed close as they rapidly inhaled each other's breath, enthusiastically saying hello. Dancer was literally trembling, unable to stand still as he shifted from foot to foot. Both were nickering with quick excitement, a low, pulsating, throaty sound, *herrherrherr*. They did this over and over and over. Finally, Dancer could no longer contend with the fence between himself and his beloved mare. He began to pace and fret. I ran to the gate that separated Dancer's pasture from the paddock where I had placed Maddy less than ten minutes before. Dancer ran through the portal and directly to Maddy's side. I stood in awe and watched as they stood together rubbing their cheeks up and down each other's neck. They were quietly nickering to each other, their eyes half closed in pure contented joy. To witness the eloquent communication between these two horses bestowed upon me an empowering gift. I was provided a furtive glance at the spiritual completeness of animals. That moment became an affirmation of the validity of Proud Spirit and its purpose.

I spent the next several days trying to research both of their pasts. It was obvious that Dancer and Maddy had known each other, but when and where? I phoned the woman who had previously owned Maddy, but she knew nothing of the mare's life before she came to them, nor could she remember the name of the people they purchased her from.

I also telephoned Marla and told her the incredible story of this reunion. Marla was just as moved as I was but could not recall a little sorrel mare with a narrow blaze and pink nose in Dancer's history. She agreed to come out and look at Maddy in person to see if she recognized her. When Marla came out to Proud Spirit to meet Maddy, she still could not place her, unfortunately, but she was thrilled for Dancer and the amazing bond he and Maddy so clearly shared. A few other leads also did not reveal any further information. If ever there was a time that I wished one of our horses could talk, this was it.

In the months and years that followed, Dancer and Maddy were absolutely inseparable. They were deeply bonded to each other, to the extent that it made some of the daily chores more time consuming. Dancer would not eat one bite of grain unless Maddy was right beside him. We tried putting them in stalls directly across from each other when Maddy first arrived, but Dancer would pace and scream till we brought Maddy in beside him. I saw no reason to ignore Dancer's need to have Maddy close, or to let him yell for her till he got over it as others told me

I should. His emotional needs had been neglected long enough, so we would faithfully indulge Dancer's devotion to Maddy. And so, from then on, they were to be fed in the same stall at the same time. This required rigging up a second bucket, and because Maddy ate faster than Dancer, we had to tie her to the opposite side of the stall, just while they ate, so she wouldn't eat Dancer's dinner after she'd finished her own.

Their attachment was even more of an inconvenience when our vet or farrier came to tend to all the horses. Unless Maddy was right beside him, Dancer simply would not stand still and would fight with us, violently throwing his head and pawing at the ground. Thankfully, both our vet and farrier were patient and good-natured enough to work around this little idiosyncrasy and didn't mind maneuvering between two horses to trim Dancer's feet or administer care.

It had been more than two years since Maddy had arrived at Proud Spirit. She and Dancer spent countless hours side by side, contentedly grazing in their lush pasture. Since their reunion, Dancer had evolved into the horse he was meant to be all along. His noble courage had always been there, of course, but now this heroic character flowed from him without effort as he became Maddy's protector. He would often position himself between her and a larger, more dominant horse. She never had to contend with the normal squabbling and dynamics of the herd because Dancer was always right there. She needed him, but much more than that, he needed her.

Maddy's arthritis was fairly severe when she came to us, but it was getting progressively worse, and we knew the time was all too rapidly approaching when we would have to make the decision to end her pain. She was lying down more frequently and for longer periods of time. She was still very interested in life and had a wonderful appetite, but she seemed to move more slowly with each passing day.

Naturally, I knew that this day would arrive, but when the afternoon came that she wouldn't get up to eat, my heart was not prepared. She had always been enthusiastic about meals. I looked out to where she quietly rested, ignoring my calls to come in for lunch, and a sickening darkness pervaded my entire body. I knew what horrific decision stood before us. I quickly tended to the others, and then went to where Maddy lay. Kneeling beside her I massaged her legs and feet while talking softly, soothing her with my voice. Dancer hovered above us. He, of course, would not leave Maddy's side and had ignored my calls for lunch as well. I tilted my face and looked up into his enormous brown eyes.

"She hurts, buddy," I said to him. "She needs us to help end her pain. And you need to let her go." I looked back to Maddy, and with a heavy heart, I scooted around from where I had been rubbing her legs up to her head. I hugged her to my chest and cupped my hand over her eye and gently closed it. "It's time," I whispered to Maddy as I held her even closer, and then looked back up to Dancer, "It's time, buddy."

I left them to call our vet, Dr. Brooks. This was not an emergency and I wanted some time to adjust to saying good-bye to Maddy and figure out how to handle Dancer. We made the appointment for a little more than a week away.

When the day arrived, there was an almost tangible feeling of oppression in the barn that made it hard to take a deep breath or even stand up straight. Jim and I loved Maddy dearly and it was going to be unbearably hard to say good-bye to her, even though we knew it was the right thing to do. Added to our despair was the underlying fear of what would happen to Dancer once she was gone. I was convinced that in mourning her loss he would simply give up.

Before we walked Maddy out to the spot where she would rest, I led her over to the stall where we had just placed Dancer. Through my tears I pleaded with Dancer to accept this and he seemed to sense what was needed of him. Just like that stormy day so long ago when we needed him to load into Carla's trailer and he obliged, he miraculously did the same thing on this day. In two years he had never once stood quietly in a stall unless Maddy was beside him, right there in the stall with him, but today he did. They stood with their noses touching over the stall door, gently nickering to each other, breathing each other's breath.

"I'm so sorry," I told them. "But you'll be together again one day, I promise." We stood there quietly, each of us absorbing the moment and dealing with this grief in our own way. Dr. Brooks arrived. "We're going to go now, Dancer, and I need you to be brave. For Maddy. Tell her good-bye, buddy." I was biting my lip. With tears streaming down my cheeks, I turned to lead her away. I silently prayed for Dancer to be calm. I didn't want Maddy's final moments on this earth to be frantic with the anguished sounds of Dancer screaming for her. I wanted this crossing to be peaceful.

Jim stayed at the barn with Dancer, to comfort him and make sure he didn't hurt himself. We were certain he would throw himself against the stall door trying to get to Maddy once she was out of his sight. But he shocked both of us by simply watching her walk away. I guess we shouldn't have been shocked, really. His brave and noble heart had already shown itself in a thousand different ways. He would once again do the right thing for Maddy. He nervously rocked back and forth from foot to foot a few times, and strained as he watched her walk away, nickering softly. But that was all. Jim stood beside him, petting his neck and talking to him, telling him it was okay. But Dancer ignored Jim and continued to nicker in a soft murmur to his beloved Maddy, his eyes riveted to the last spot he saw her.

At the back of our property, under a glorious old oak tree, I held Maddy's head close to my chest and kissed her between the ears. And then, like I had done so many times in the past, I cupped my hands over her eyes and told her I loved her. She gently relaxed against me, and I nodded for Dr. Brooks to proceed.

When this precious little horse slipped from my arms, we heard an unmistakable high-pitched whinny from the barn. Jim said it was the only time Dancer called out.

I prayed that Maddy's final breath was carried on the wind to envelop Dancer in peace and serenity, letting him know she was okay. She was no longer in pain . . . and she would be waiting. ♘

Inseparable after their reunion, Dancer and Maddy share a pan of apples and carrots.

Gambler

THE CALL FINALLY CAME AROUND EIGHT IN THE EVENING.

"Hi, Mel, it's Andie."

"Andie! Is everything okay? Is he on the way?" I asked.

"Yeah, they left about an hour ago. Should get to your place sometime 'round ten."

"Great!" I said. "I've been going crazy wondering what's going on." I didn't know her very well, and in fact we'd never even met—just talked on the phone a few times—but she sounded strained and preoccupied. I could hear her take several deep breaths as I spoke, and my voice trailed off, waiting.

"Yeah, I would've called sooner, but it's been a little crazy around here." She let out a small humorless laugh, then added, "I've been trying to save my job."

"What do you mean you're trying to save your job? What happened?" I was concerned about whatever trouble Andie was going through, and she clearly sounded upset, but at this point it was Mac finally being on the road to Proud Spirit that was foremost in my mind.

Andie took another deep breath. She started to speak, but her voice cracked and she stopped to catch her breath once again.

"What is it, Andie?"

"Oh, Mel, I had no choice! You're gonna kill me!" She started to cry openly, as all sorts of awful thoughts about what could have possibly happened swirled around inside my head. I assured Andie that it was fine and prodded her to tell me what was wrong. Little did I know that Andie's trouble at work would translate into my giving much more to this arrangement than we had originally agreed upon.

Andie is in her mid-fifties and is the divorced mother of two grown kids. She works at a Thoroughbred racetrack here in Florida as a groom, and occasionally rides young horses in training. The job accomplishes two things: it keeps her head above water—barely—and, more importantly, it allows her to be near horses.

She had called me more than a month before, asking if we could take in a retired horse that she had taken care of, off and on, for almost ten years. McGee, or Mac for short, had been owned by one man for most of his racing career. In the context of these small low-purse tracks scattered all across the United States, the big bay Thoroughbred had won a decent amount of money. When Mac's owner and his horses were on the racing circuit and made their way back to the track where Andie worked, it was usually she who was hired to be the horse's groom and warm-up jockey. Over the years Andie had come to love Mac as if he were her own. After many years of giving his best to his owner, the gelding suffered a leg injury that would ultimately end his career.

In the very first days of the expected months and months that Mac would need to recover, before it was determined that he would never race again, he was put in Andie's full-time care. She devoted herself to him completely and followed the veterinarian's instructions to the letter. He was only twelve at the time—young for most horses, but old for a Thoroughbred that had been raced hard on the track for so many years. His age, coupled with the severity of the injury, made it clear that a full recovery was not to be.

One afternoon, Mac's owner came to the track and informed Andie that he was going to be selling the horse to slaughter. Andie was devastated. This happy, beautiful boy who was still playful, who would willingly lower his head for kisses, who preferred apples over carrots, and who had given and given and given till he could give no more was going to end up standing in the manure, urine, and blood of the horses that came before him in line at the slaughterhouse. His final memory would be the sickening stench of fear and death that had permeated itself into the concrete floor as a retractable bullet shattered his skull. Andie pleaded with the man not to send him off to this horrific fate. "I can't keep paying for a horse that's not bringing in any money," he told her.

Andie convinced him to sell Mac to her for a couple of hundred dollars less than he would get from the killers. She paid him partially in cash, with money she could scarcely spare, and the rest she worked off by tending his horses without pay till the debt was settled. Andie moved Mac to a friend's house on ten acres where he spent the next few years as a companion to her friend's mare.

Mac became very attached to his new companion and the peaceful life away from the track, a life where he could actually touch another horse—something so simple, yet essential to a horse's emotional well-being—where he wasn't stuck in a windowless stall for twenty-four hours a day, seven days a week. He could move around his pasture, breathe fresh air, and eat grass or roll in the sand. He could rest soundly and not be startled by the constant noise and rushing activity that took place all hours of the day and night at the track.

But life was still not settled for this special Thoroughbred.

Andie's friend told her she needed to move Mac. They were sell-ing their small farm and their mare and moving back into town. Andie had no choice but to bring Mac back to the racetrack and put him in an empty stall till she could find another place to board him that she could afford. Andie had tears in her eyes as she drove him out the driveway of her friend's house, away from this idyllic life that had been so brief. She could hear him kicking the back of the trailer in frustration. He called to his beloved companion as the distraught mare ran along the fence line with the departing trailer, screaming for Mac to be returned to her side. Andie made a vow then and there that she would find him a home where he could live for the rest of his life. He would not be ripped away ever again from a horse with whom he had formed a bond. He would live in peace and dignity, immersed in the security of a herd, overseen by people who believed in pre-serving a horse's spirit. And so it was that Andie eventually heard of Proud Spirit and got in touch with me.

The night Andie called me to let me know Mac was on his way, I had to reassure her many times before she could tell me what was wrong.

"I was at the track, standing around with Mac at his stall, saying good-bye to him and all that, ya know, just waiting on the hauler to come pick him up and bring him down to you," she finally began.

As she had stood near the end of the forty-stall barn where Mac was being kept, she recognized one of the trainers who worked for a very wealthy man enter the center aisle way from the opposite end of the barn. He had with him a pure black Thoroughbred gelding named Gambler. Andie knew this horse well. He was a frequent top winner and had brought in more money than most horses at this track. But, like so many others, he had been pushed too hard too young, and he suffered hairline fractures in both knees. The owner wanted this powerful, high-spirited moneymaker back on the track as soon as possible. Andie had spoken to the trainer frequently about Gambler's recovery, and the man was always pessimistic, saying what a waste of time it was and that the horse would never race again. "I'll get it through that ignorant owner's head soon enough to get rid of this dead weight," he would angrily say.

Sadly, the trainer was right. Gambler wasn't given enough time to heal and his performance was never the same. Every day Gambler's abusive trainer would push him on the track, driving him into a pounding run when he should have been resting his fractured knees, and every day Gambler would turn in a slower and slower time. After these disappointing training sessions, once the trainer had Gambler unsaddled and back in the barn, he would beat the horse into a frenzy with an unyielding whip, violently slashing him across the neck and shoulders as punishment for "not trying."

Weeks and weeks of irrational abuse finally took their toll on Gambler, and he could take no more. Out of self-preservation, the horse started to fight back. Now, as the man would approach the barn with Gambler, the horse would start to dangerously kick out and throw his body sideways in anticipation of the violent beatings. This powerful, elegant athlete had been destroyed physically, but the trainer couldn't stop there. He had to try to murder his spirit as well.

Andie had been watching from the aisle way as Gambler fought to keep from entering the barn. He knew what awaited. Gambler would not move forward, so, with unwarranted hostility, the trainer turned him around and was trying to back him in, already beating him across the neck. Gambler's eyes were wild and he was soaked in sweat—the sweat of fear, anger, and exhaustion, having given everything he had to give just moments before on the track. And then it happened.

In a rage, the powerful gelding reared up to his full height, and snorting through flared nostrils he stormed at his abuser on massive hind legs, striking out at the trainer's head with his lethal front hooves. In the course of a few weeks, Gambler had gone from being a horse who willingly did whatever was asked of him to being one who feared humans so intensely he hated them. He had crossed that line and was hitting back with more vehemence than he had ever put into running.

The infuriated trainer began beating Gambler across the stomach with a long whip. Numerous bystanders watched him but simply shook their heads and walked away. It is a rare person who will intervene on a horse's behalf at these facilities, where making money is the number one priority. But when Andie saw what happened, she left Mac's side and ran down the aisle of the barn. When she reached the trainer, he was out of breath and obviously livid. Gambler had dropped down so all four feet were on the ground now, but he was still fighting the restraints and was visibly shaken.

"What are you doing!" she shouted. "Why are you hitting him!"

"Why don't you mind your own business," he said through clenched teeth, still wrestling with the frightened horse.

"Stop it!" Andie snapped. He acted like he didn't hear her. "Stop it now!" she yelled. "Or I'll call the steward and see that you're banned from ever working here again."

He turned abruptly to face her. "Who the hell do you think you are? You don't have that kind of power."

"Maybe I don't, but those welts do," she stated flatly, pointing to the horse's flank that revealed every torturous slash of the whip.

The trainer threw Gambler's lead rope at Andie, threatening, "Get that filthy bastard out of my sight or I'll take him out back and shoot him." Andie turned and trotted a willing Gambler out and away from the barn to a patch of grass to let the horse calm down.

The man who was going to be hauling Mac to Proud Spirit had arrived at the track during the ruckus, but he was indifferent, busily unloading horses he had just brought in and putting others that were being moved to different destinations on the trailer.

Moments later, Gambler's trainer regained his composure and came out to get the horse from Andie. He looked her in the eye as he reached for the lead rope and said, "This horse is out of here today. And trust me, he won't be breathing when he leaves. Got it? Don't ever tell me how to handle a horse again."

Andie decided to follow her instincts about intervening on behalf of this horse and moved her hand holding the lead rope away from the man's reach. "If you don't think he's ever going to race again, go get me his papers and I'll put him on that trailer right there," she said to the trainer as she turned and pointed to the slick aluminum eight-horse gooseneck trailer sitting in the parking lot at the end of the barn. "I'll save you a whole bunch of hassle and you'll never have to see him again." Gambler's owner was telephoned and told of Gambler's declining performance—including the dangerous display of defiance he had put on this day and the ensuing battle of words between Andie and the trainer. The owner simply said, "Get rid of him."

"He's on the trailer with Mac, Mel!" Andie nervously said over the phone. "He's coming to Proud Spirit. I didn't know what else to do! The guy was really going to shoot him! He was going to take him out back and shoot him!"

"Andie . . . I . . . Oh, geez. What am I going to do with him . . . " I stammered.

"I didn't know what else to do! My boss is furious at me for interfering." Andie started to cry again.

"Listen, it's all right. You did the right thing. It's just that he sounds like a real handful. Oh, boy."

"The horses are here, Hon. The trailer's just pulling in," Jim said as he gently shook my shoulder. I had fallen asleep on the couch—it was just after midnight.

I grabbed a sweatshirt and pulled it over my head as I walked outside. It was November and the evenings were a little chilly now. Jim and I stood in the driveway watching the long diesel pickup truck with the shiny aluminum trailer in tow pull up to our barn. When the rig came to a stop, a huge, stocky man wearing black jeans and a white T-shirt emerged from the cab. I had stepped forward to introduce myself. He had a cigarette in his mouth and another one tucked behind his ear, and he stank of stale smoke and foul sweat. I told him my name and thanked him for bringing the horses safely. He didn't offer his own name or acknowledge my thanks, but instead hiked his drooping jeans up over his pronounced belly as he surveyed our midnight-darkened pastures, and exclaimed, "Woooweee! You folks is out in the *boonies!* I didn't think I was ever gonna come up on yer place."

"We were wondering if you had some trouble. We expected you around ten," I said.

"Yeah, well, I had a few stops to make," he offered as he blew smoke from his lungs.

I could hear the horses shuffling around inside the trailer over the loud rumble of the truck's diesel engine. The trailer was full, and one of the horses was blowing great bursts of air nervously through his nostrils. Every few seconds one of them kicked the aluminum side of the trailer.

The driver looked toward the sound. "Where're these guys goin'? I want that one little S.O.B. outta my new trailer 'fore he dents it all to hell." He started walking briskly to the rear of the trailer.

"Um, they're going in this paddock here, I guess," I told him as I pointed behind the barn.

The man stopped abruptly and turned back to look at me. "I'd put 'em in a stall if I were you."

"Why?" I asked.

"'Cause they don't know nothin' else, that's why. You gonna take horses that're both over ten years old who've never been turned out with another horse or spent more 'n a few minutes of their life on grass and jus' let 'em go? That's jus' crazy, lady.

These horses don' know how to act like horses. You'd be wise to remember that."

I refrained from getting into a discussion with him, and he obviously didn't know that Mac had had some real horse time at Andie's friends. I simply told him that was fine, and I'd put them in a stall.

The man led Mac off first. The big bay gelding backed out of the trailer and was fairly calm, his head high in the air as he sniffed his new surroundings. I reached up to pet his neck when suddenly a thunderous crashing came from inside the trailer, startling both Mac and me, followed by an ear-shattering, screaming whinny that echoed through the night and then oddly quieted down into a rumbling growl. I couldn't recall ever hearing a horse actually growl, and I nervously looked to Jim, my brows knitted together in concern.

Slam! Slam! Slam! Once again, hooves crashing against the side of the trailer over and over and over. In between those pounding kicks and those horrible guttural screams, the horse I assumed was Gambler kept blowing reverberating blasts of air through his flared nostrils. The noise this one horse was making was unbelievable.

The man quickly handed me Mac's lead rope and said, "Here! Get him back so I can get that little S.O.B. outta my trailer."

I passed the lead rope on to Jim. He was shaking his head at the man's harshness, but started walking Mac to the barn. *Slam! Slam! Slam!* And then that guttural scream again from inside the trailer. The man angrily spat the cigarette from his mouth and heaved his bulk up into the trailer. He threw aside the divider that held Gambler in place, and it crashed, metal on metal against the side of the trailer. The noise scared Gambler, who was already very close to exploding, and the terrified horse lunged forward, slamming into the front wall. Then, just as quickly, he backed up like a freight train, bucking out at the sidewall, grunting loudly with the effort it took as each blast of his feet dented the trailer wall.

"Get back!" the man yelled at me. He grabbed a whip that

was clipped into the corner of the trailer.

"Don't hit him!" I hollered. The man ignored me. He reached forward and struck Gambler on the chest to make him back up. The horse wasn't positioned right and his fear of the whip only made him slam into the side of the trailer and kick out. The man brought the whip down between Gambler's legs and in quick succession brought it back up against his stomach as hard as he could. Gambler shuffled to get away from the weapon, to no avail. At the resounding slap of the whip on his skin, the horse put his head down and loudly snorted like an enraged bull, violently pawing the floor of the trailer. Then, suddenly, he brought his head back up, tucked his chin, and tried to rear. The confines of the trailer prevented this, and I thought he was going to go through the roof.

"Stop it!" I yelled at the man. "Let him calm down!"

"He can calm down in hell," he hissed through gritted teeth, and continued to try to maneuver the horse by hitting him with the whip.

The horse's huge feet crashed back to the floor and he roared in frustration. My eyes were wide with horror, mirroring Gambler's own eyes, which were rimmed in white, as I watched from a safe distance at the open doors of the trailer.

I'd never seen such fury in an animal. He looked insane and my heart was breaking for him. My God! I thought. How am I ever going to get through to him! I've never handled anything like this in my life!

"Back up, you little son of a bitch!" the man yelled as he hit Gambler on the chest again. Once again, this only made the horse slam into the side wall. This time the man completely lost his temper. His face was beet red, he was out of breath, and the veins on his neck stood out. He raised the whip to the roof of the trailer and brought it down across Gambler's face.

"Stop it!" I screamed. Jim came running out of the barn to intervene just as Gambler exploded out of the trailer. The man flattened himself against the side to avoid being crushed, and he managed to grab the lead rope as the frenzied horse flew by him. The man jumped out of the trailer, keeping hold of the rope as Gambler found his footing and finally stopped moving backward. The horse stood pawing and snorting. He was soaked in sweat and his entire body was trembling, as if he wanted to flee.

"Jesus Christ," I breathed out. "What do you people do to these horses . . ."

This was rhetorical and I didn't really want an answer from him—in fact, I just wanted this guy off my property. He was still out of breath but no longer angry, and he looked at me with a cocky, self-satisfied grin on his face, as if this barbaric scene we'd just witnessed was fun sport for him, and said, "We make 'em wanna run, lady. Make 'em wanna run."

Jim already had Mac secure in a stall, and I walked Gambler into the paddock with the intention of placing him in a stall as well. The horse was throwing his head and still snorting as he nervously trotted sideways at the end of his lead rope. I had foolishly forgotten what Andie had told me about the beatings at the racetrack during the last two weeks of Gambler's life, and when we approached the barn he reacted with the same fearful defensiveness in anticipation of being beaten.

He had only set one hoof on the concrete when he threw his head, pulled back and reared up with startling force. I held onto the lead rope, but kept every inch of its six-foot length between Gambler's lethal hooves and my soft head. When he dropped back down to all fours, I allowed him to move away from the barn so he could calm down. After a short period of time, I managed to walk him into a stall with relative ease and was confident that he would settle in shortly. I slipped the halter from his head, stepped back into the aisle way and closed the door.

But I was dead wrong about that. I'm not sure what set him

off, but as soon as the latch was in place Gambler seemed to go berserk. He began running in circles around the tight confines of the stall. With each turn he slowed down just enough to blast out with both back feet against the wall as he let out an ear-piercing scream, over and over again.

I stood incredulous, and was heartsick that he should be so emotionally distraught and physically riled. I decided that if he had this much energy to burn, he needed some space to run. Ignoring the hauler's advice, I opened the stall door, stood back, and let him run out to the paddock. Mac had become agitated during Gambler's display, and I let him out into the pitch black of night as well.

I could hear their pounding hooves as they ran the perimeter of the paddock. I could hear their massive lungs rapidly sucking in oxygen. In another situation, in another time or place, these sounds may have been reminiscent of the enduring spirit of the horse, the sounds of freedom. But not this night, not now, for this was the sound of fervent anguish. I turned back to the house, shaking my head at the sadness of it all, and went to bed.

The following morning I awoke early and threw on some jeans, then headed outside. I was anxious to get acquainted with Mac and Gambler. I found them peacefully dozing under a tree in the small paddock where I had turned them out the night before. I stood watching for a moment. They noticed me at the same time and lifted their heads ever so slightly to look in my direction.

"Hi, guys!" I called out. They stared for just a moment, then looked away unconcerned and once again lowered their heads. I started walking out to them. As I approached, Gambler calmly backed up, putting some distance between us. Mac nickered softly and moved forward to say hello. I reached up to rub his forehead and asked him if he was ready for some breakfast. When I peeked around Mac's shoulder and asked Gambler the same thing, he backed up even farther at the sound of my voice.

"It's all right, buddy. We'll take it slow," I assured him, and then walked back to the barn with Mac following closely behind.

I led Mac into a stall and looked out to see if Gambler was coming on his own. He still stood under the tree but watched us carefully. I gave Mac his grain, and then shook a bucket with more grain in it for Gambler, trying to entice him to come in and eat. He turned to the sound and began walking toward the barn.

The morning sun was just coming over the stand of pine trees behind Gambler's back, its subtle pink glow illuminating his black coat. I was more familiar with the numerous elderly horses that resided at our sanctuary—their slow gentle step, their coats slightly dulled with age, their muscles slack from little demand. But this horse walking toward me now was pure power and muscle from the rigors of hard work. His coat glistened like oil from spending so much time in a stall and never being out in the sun.

I pushed open the first stall door and stood back. Gambler tentatively stepped into the barn, sniffed the concrete, then lifted his head high and blew a blast of air through his nostrils as he surveyed his surroundings. He seemed to be calmer without the restraint of a halter and with my keeping a distance. It was a very peaceful morning, and the only sound was that of Mac munching his grain. I felt certain that Gambler could sense the difference in atmosphere here at Proud Spirit compared to the frenetic activity of the barn at the track.

"Easy, son," I spoke gently. "Go on in the stall and eat your breakfast."

The huge horse seemed to look right through me as he brusquely strode past me and the stall door I had left open for him. When he reached the end of the aisle way he leaned down to the gate there and shoved it hard with his nose, taking the slack out of the chain that held the gate closed with a loud clang. I stood watching, not saying a word. He shoved the gate again.

Quickly bored with that, Gambler turned around and defiantly looked out the back of the barn. Drawing himself up to his full height, he stood still and once again blew a loud burst of air through his nostrils, trumpeting his arrival. I kept thinking how huge and powerful he looked. And for that very reason, I decided this was enough posturing on his part. He was too massive and cocky for me to let him display even one moment of dominant behavior over me—which he was already doing by ignoring my presence. I stepped behind him to make myself known and gently waved him into the stall.

Even though he was well out of my reach, as I safely kept my distance and made a point to keep my movements calm and slow, Gambler skittered nervously into the stall and towards the grain waiting there to avoid my extended arm. "You're not such a tough guy," I told him as I closed the door.

While Mac and Gambler were eating, I decided to place them in a small four-acre pasture by themselves until I got to know them better and figured out how I was going to integrate them into the herd.

I slipped a halter over Mac's head to lead him out. He was an amiable fellow and I could see why Andie loved him so. At the gate of his new pasture, I took the halter off and let him go. He called out a hello, to see what sort of reply he'd get from our other horses, I presumed. There was none forthcoming, and he trotted to the far fence line to try again. He seemed content enough, and was just getting to know the territory. I left the gate open and walked back up to the barn to retrieve Gambler.

As I approached I could hear he was agitated. He was snorting and rapidly pacing in front of his door. "What's wrong, Gambler? Take it easy, son." I tried to console him as I slid back the latch on the stall door. I barely had the door open when he charged the outlet. I stomped my foot and swung the halter I still carried in my hand at his chest. He immediately retreated and stood watching me. I backed him up a few more steps by squaring my shoulders and shaking the halter at his chest to try and establish some dominance. He was astonishingly aggressive, but I could not let him move me out of his way or I would never be able to safely control him. He backed up a few steps, and again stood watching me with wary eyes.

126

I relaxed my posture, lowered the halter, and approached. He nervously bobbed his head up and down but then let me step beside him and I reached up to rub his forehead. I slipped the halter on easily and continued to rub his head and ears. He didn't seem to like, or understand, my touch. He kept alternating between relaxing and nervously bobbing his head. I didn't want to put too much on him, so I chose a moment of calm to stop touching him.

"Okay big guy, are you ready to go hang out with Mac and learn how to be a horse?" I asked him as I pushed open the stall door to lead him out of the barn.

The moment all four feet were on the concrete Gambler startled me by letting out an anguished groan and rearing straight up. I was directly under him and when I turned all I saw was six feet of belly and flashing hooves. In one movement I swung to the side just as he came crashing down. He threw his head from side to side, trying to rid himself of the restraints of the halter, and then sprang up and down as if he were going to rear again.

There was no way I could safely lead this horse in the state he was in, and I reached up to pull the halter off with the intention of letting him go. The muscles in his neck were hard and taught with the strain of his determination to get away from me. I quickly unlatched the lead rope at the same time that I tried to pull the halter off. But I was too late. He felt the freedom I had allowed and reared up once again. My hand was on the halter as he pulled away, and all I managed to do was pull it off one side of his head. With that, he came back down as I pivoted out of his way. The giant horse turned on his haunches and was gone out the back of the barn.

In a pounding run Gambler circled the paddock, then found the open gate of the pasture and tore through the opening to join Mac. I was in absolute awe as I watched him galloping across the pasture. He was simply stunning—to the point that he made me forget all his dangerous antics from just moments before.

I couldn't help but envision this horse in the days and weeks to come. I wondered how his personality would emerge as he learned to trust and as he and I formed a relationship. I had no doubt that he would trust again. I knew this because of something that is very hard to define, one of those remarkable, intangible things we can see in a horse's eyes if only we would look. If only we would see.

I was suddenly overcome with a peaceful assurance that he would show me how to indemnify all the wrong that had been done to him. And I felt confident that once he understood what we offered, he would allow himself this partnership with us, for he had already proven his intelligence and shown his immense heart through all that he had given in his lifetime.

After a moment, I shook my head, clearing the reverie, and concentrated on the problem at hand. Somehow, that halter had stayed half on and half off his head as he galloped to join Mac, and I needed to get it off. It's dangerous enough to turn a horse out with a halter on that fits properly. If the halter got caught on a tree limb or a fence post, a determined horse could break his neck. But this was even worse—the throat latch was dangling down to create more of an unsafe situation.

At first, I tried the obvious and easiest tactic—luring him to me with food. Unfortunately, he had just eaten and wasn't interested in the least. I'm not sure he would have come to me even if he was hungry. Aside from the fact that he had already expressed his disdain of humans when he reared up at me in the barn, the wide-open freedom of this four-acre pasture was something new to this horse and he was enthusiastically investigating the grass and trees. I was the last thing on his mind now.

To get this halter off before he hurt himself, I would have to communicate with Gambler like a more dominant horse would. Horses are herd animals—they need the security that numbers provide. If I stood near Mac and drove Gambler away from us, I would in essence be establishing myself as the alpha horse in this herd of three. And near the alpha, or dominant, horse is the safest place to be. So by controlling his movement, or driving him out of the herd, I would be setting up a chain of events in Gambler's mind that would result in his simply wanting to be allowed back in, to be near me.

I walked out to the pasture with a length of eight-foot, soft cotton rope to act as an extension of my arm. If he simply walked away from my approach, I would make him trot away by tossing the rope at his rump. If he trotted away, I'd make him run by tossing the rope harder. To a bystander, it would appear that Gambler was achieving his goal—he wanted to keep his distance, and at the onset that's what he was doing. But by making him move faster than he wanted, he would soon get the message that I was controlling his movement, which in turn would communicate to him that I was dominant.

When we take in a horse that we are told is hard to catch, it usually takes about ten minutes of working with him like this to cure the problem. Sometimes up to a half hour. But like so many thousands of other horses who had been bred to run, Gambler had never been properly socialized with other horses. And even though thousands of years of instincts would dictate his behavior, he still wasn't sure what it meant to be driven from the herd. It took almost two exhausting hours for Gambler to walk up to me, asking to be allowed back into the herd, so I could remove the halter dangling from his head.

At first, when I approached and he moved away and I tossed the rope at him to move him away faster, he looked at me as an irritation, a disruption of his grazing. And after an hour and a half of moving him around on four acres and of his still regarding me as an irritation, I genuinely started to wonder if this concept would work with him. Even though it was November and the evenings can be rather cool then, the days are still hot in Florida. Just as the blistering sun was starting to take its toll on me—I was soaked with sweat, out of breath, my legs were screaming from bounding through the high grass—Gambler turned and faced me. For nearly an hour and a half he had kept his back to me, but finally, he faced me.

I immediately rewarded him by stopping my pursuit, relaxing my posture, dropping my head, and turning away from him. All this was telling him he was welcome to step into my space. He could approach. Gambler tentatively bobbed his head up and down and then took a few cautious steps toward me. I encouraged him by keeping my head down, and moving back ever so slightly. Suddenly, he drew himself up, thrust his chin at me, and in a clear challenge, he turned from me and trotted away.

With a groan, I squared my shoulders and briskly stepped after him, tossing the rope at his rump to make him move faster. He picked up his pace to avoid the rope, then instantly came to a stop and faced me once again. And once again, I quickly dropped my shoulders and turned away to invite him to come closer, whispering through my ragged breath over and over, "Please, please, please, come to me, buddy."

I saw the breakthrough this time. Gambler's eyes softened and he began working his mouth, or chewing, something horses do when they figure something out. He gently bobbed his head up and down, just as before, and took the same tentative steps in my direction. I continued to welcome him to come closer with my body language. When he moved to within a few feet from me I took a step and closed the gap, keeping my head down and my shoulders angled to the side. When I stood within inches, I turned directly to him and smiled into his eyes. Gambler lowered his head and gently blew a few times through his nostrils. I leaned down, my mouth almost touching his muzzle, and blew back, saying hello, and then we simply looked at each other.

"That's all I wanted, buddy," I quietly told him as I reached up and rubbed his forehead. He pulled back from my touch but mercifully stayed his ground. I set my hand on his neck, and then slipped the offending halter from his head. I looked him in the eye for few more moments, and through the lump in my throat I smiled when I saw the hardness soften. Then I left him.

The following days and weeks proved to be one of the most rewarding experiences of my life. This horse, who just weeks before only wanted to crush his handlers, was becoming as gentle as a kitten. In a very short time he allowed me to hug his head to my chest and cup my hands over his eyes as I gently rubbed them closed. He would sigh contentedly and lean his weight against me while a myriad of emotions blurred my vision with tears. I couldn't help but think about where his life might have gone, and I was so deeply grateful that we were blessed with the opportunity to give this remarkable horse a chance to know a kind hand. Gambler's generous heart, and his willingness to trust after all he had endured, are a testament to the pure and genuine spirit of all horses. I am thankful that we are able to offer him a dignified and deserved life of peace at Proud Spirit.

Gambler now spends his days contentedly frolicking and romping with four other horses on a fifteen-acre pasture of lush grass. He will never again feel the slash of a whip. ♘

Dusty, Gambler, Sammy, and Cleveland Brown

Sugar and the Fireflies

I MUST HAVE DRIVEN BY THIS PASTURE A THOUSAND TIMES. It was on the way to and from the feed store where I bought the grain and other essentials for my horses. But "pasture" isn't really the right word for the patch of land. That word conjures up an image of lush grass with maybe a spattering of oak trees for shade. This was more like a five-acre jungle. It was overgrown with weeds as tall as a house and scrub so thick you couldn't see farther than thirty feet back. I don't believe there was a single blade of grass on the entire five acres. Across the front of the property there was a rickety, falling-down fence strung with barbed wire hanging loosely here and there. I had never seen a horse on this property nor any activity at all from anyone who may possibly have owned it.

I was on my way home from doing errands in town and had been absentmindedly ticking off the chores that I hoped to accomplish this day. As I came around the curve just before the ramshackle lot, my eye caught something that was out of place within its boundaries. I was completely taken aback to see a horse.

My surprise to see the animal standing up near the front of the property immediately turned to horror when I saw the condition the little sorrel mare was in. Barely believing my own eyes, I slowed my truck to a stop and pulled over to the side of the road. Jim and I had been taking in abused horses for quite a few years, but I had never seen anything like this. She was so severely emaciated I truly did not know how she was standing. I got out of my truck and walked over to the gate but noticed it was chained and locked. I was so shocked at her condition, I kept muttering "Oh, my God" to myself over and over slowly, almost involuntarily.

I found myself looking up and down the road, as if I needed another person to confirm what stood before me, but I guess it was more of a reflex to the shock I felt than anything else. We live in a rural area, and this starving horse and I were alone. I spread apart a couple strands of the barbed wire so I could crawl through them and go to her side. She slowly turned her head to me and nickered so weakly I wasn't even sure I heard it.

Gently, I rested my hand on her neck and told her it was going to be okay, although in my heart I wasn't sure it would be. She was wasted away to nearly nothing and would not survive much longer without immediate intervention. Even then, I still wasn't sure she could be brought back to good health. If she was so far gone that her internal organs had been compromised, then immediate intervention was even more essential, for euthanasia would be more humane than allowing her to painfully starve to death.

I wanted to quickly assess her condition, so I ran my hand along her jutting spine. Her dull sparse coat was pulled tight across her bones and felt lifeless to my touch. When she cocked her hip to rest on the other leg it seemed as though her hipbone was going to come through the skin. I continued around to her backside and lifted her tail. The lack of muscle caused her flesh to simply hang, and there was an eight- to ten-inch gap where healthy, strong haunches should have been rubbing together.

I kept shaking my head, tears welling in my eyes as once

again I tried to comprehend what sort of person could do this. How could this happen? I was outraged and infuriated, but I quickly told myself what a waste of time that was. It's really not such a mystery—the reality of this life here on earth is that from time to time we will encounter horrors such as this starving mare and things that are much, much worse. There is no escaping this. Disturbing things have been happening since the beginning of time, they happen now, and will happen for all eternity. So, I told myself, it is a waste of energy to ask how this could happen. The focus of our energy should go towards changing the fate of those who suffer as a consequence.

Making my way back up to the little mare's head I gently rubbed her forehead. And looking into her tired starving eyes, searching there, I tried to glean the intangible: her will to live. I kept taking deep breaths as I tried to swallow the lump in my throat. My shoulders sagged with the burden of emotions brought on just by looking at this poor horse. I was overtaken with a powerful sadness that went to the core of my heart.

All the while, my head was churning as I tried to figure out how I was going to get her to Proud Spirit. The back of my truck was filled with grain, as I was just coming from the feed store. I ripped open a bag, then took as much as I could cup in my hands to her. She dove in happily and finished every bit of it. I smiled to see that at least she still had an appetite, which was a good sign. I stood in front of her, looking into her liquid brown eyes as she licked my hands, and I tried to decide what to do.

Did I want to get law enforcement involved? Or try the friendly-neighbor approach? I had learned that being non-con-frontational usually worked best. I would somehow get the name and phone number of the abusive owner and give him a call, say-ing something along the lines of "I see you have a horse on your property that no one is really using. I'm looking for a companion for an elderly horse of mine and was wondering if you would be interested in parting with the mare (or gelding, or donkey, or whatever)." This works beautifully in the right situation. Never mentioning the deplorable condition of the poor animals and being willing to pay money often helps to rescue them from their situation.

Someone once asked me how I deal with not seeing the abusive owners of the horses I have rescued punished. Why is it enough for me just to get the horse away from them? Shouldn't they pay for what they've done? Shouldn't they be taught a lesson? All I can say is that, for me, this isn't about the people—it's about the horses. I don't have the time, the inclination, or the energy to try and show these fools the error of their ways. I truly believe that people are either inherently good or bad. I have done things in my life that I am not proud of while in a bad mood. Who hasn't? But that's not my character, or who I am deep down inside. I believe I'm a good person. I believe most people are good.

But the person who owns a horse and allows her to slowly starve to death the way this horse was, and doesn't think that is wrong? That person is nothing less than evil. There is something deeply wrong with his or her intrinsic self that goes way beyond having a bad day. And there isn't anything that I, or anyone else, could ever say or do to make someone this ignorant, callous, and insensitive change. Short of some life-altering event, this is who this person is—evil. And I believe that ultimately, he or she will be punished.

My friends who know me well know how I talk to the animals in my life. Beyond the idle chatter, when a situation is difficult or emotional, I always tell the horses what is happening. It helps me to verbalize our relationship; we somehow stay more connected. And I did that now. I hugged the little mare's head as I told her everything would work out. I told her she was going to come to Proud Spirit where she would be fed, loved, and taken care of for the rest of her life. If she was simply too tired to fight anymore, then we would accept this and we would help her cross over, peacefully and humanely. And I promised her I would be back in a few hours to give her some dinner. I crawled back through the barbed wire and sat in my truck for a minute trying to think of what to do next.

Just then I saw a woman pulling into her drive at the property next door. Quickly, I started up my truck and pulled in behind her. Her property seemed to be about five acres also, except there was a small but very nice home set back from the road, with an inviting, shady front porch across the front of the house. There were two slick and shiny horses grazing in the lush, grassy pasture and they trotted over to the well-kept fence line as the woman and I both got out of our trucks at the same time. She looked to be about my age and had a friendly and welcoming smile. I introduced myself and told her I lived a few miles down on the next cross road. She told me her name was Doreen.

I decided to watch what I said till I knew more. After all, maybe the horse next door was hers, maybe the mare was just really elderly and had been very ill, and that's why she was separated from the others—I'd never looked in the horse's mouth to see how old she might be. Or maybe they had just rescued the little mare from someplace else and that's why I had never seen her before.

Anyway, all I said was that I was driving by and had never seen that mare before, as I pointed across the way, and that I was concerned. Even though you couldn't see another home from where we stood, and Doreen and I were completely alone, she lowered her voice and took a step closer to me. "Isn't it awful?" she said. "She belongs to a man that lives in town, a Mr. Land. I don't think he cares about her at all. I take hay over there now and then and throw it over the fence for her. He usually keeps her penned up on about an acre in the back, but it's nothing but sand there. That's why you've never seen her. She must have gotten out, because he sure never lets her out."

"Are you friends with him?" I asked.

"Oh, no, we see him now and then when he comes out here once in a while and we wave, that's about it. About a week ago he asked my husband if he would mow over there for him, knock down the weeds, he said."

I asked her if she had ever said anything to him about the

condition of the horse. Doreen said that she did say something once and all Mr. Land would say was that the horse was really old and didn't eat too well. Doreen also said that she wanted to do something to help the mare, but was even nervous about throwing her hay because Mr. Land seemed a little strange and she wouldn't want to be on his bad side.

I could hear the trepidation in Doreen's voice as she told me all this, and I wondered what obstacles I was going to encounter in trying to get this horse away from Mr. Land. In light of everything she had revealed about the situation, I felt free to talk to Doreen and told her that we had a horse sanctuary nearby and that I would like to bring the mare home. Doreen was excited and relieved that someone wanted to get involved and we talked about the best way to handle it. She felt certain that if we caused Mr. Land any trouble or accused him of mistreating the horse it would be worse for the mare and possibly for us as well.

She confided in me that she thought he was probably a pretty nasty person with a bad temper, not only because of the condition of this horse, but also because of certain things he had ranted to Doreen's husband about, things that she felt a normal person wouldn't go on about. But she liked my idea of saying that someone just wanted the mare as a companion for another horse, and Doreen offered to call him for me later that evening. We exchanged phone numbers and I continued on home. Doreen said she would call the minute she had some news.

A few hours later I brought another small serving of grain back down to the mare and while she ate out of the bucket I held for her, I told her that we had started the ball rolling and she would be safe soon. I saw Doreen outside with her own horses and we waved and smiled at each other. We barely knew each other, yet I felt as though we were partners and shared the goal of saving this little horse.

Before the mare had finished her dinner a man came by in a black pickup. He had a thick gray beard peppered with black where the gray hadn't yet completely taken over. Tipped back off his forehead he wore a felt cowboy hat, the brim stained with dirt and sweat. He stopped his truck where I was standing with the mare and let out a short, affected laugh while he asked, "Somebody finally gonna do somethin' about that poor horse?"

"I'm hoping that Mr. Land will let me have her," I said. "Do you know him?"

"Yeah, I work with him once in a while over on this ranch." He jerked his head to the right, indicating the ranch across the street. He shook his head and chuckled again, "He's a sorry son of a bitch, but I hope he lets you have her. Why do you want her, anyway?"

"Oh, I just like horses." I said with a smile, and he drove off with a wave.

About eight o'clock that evening the phone rang and I picked up. "Melanie?" an excited voice spoke into my ear.

"Yes . . . ," I said.

"This is Doreen. He said you can have her!"

"Oh, thank goodness! I'll call my vet first thing in the morning and get him out there to pull blood for a Coggins test and give her a once-over. While we wait for the blood work I'm going to start taking her small amounts of grain three or four times a day. I can't wait to get her home! Thank you, Doreen!" We hung up and I excitedly told Jim that Mr. Land said we could have her. He laughed at me and said he guessed that from my conversation. I wished out loud that we had a place on our own property to put her where she would be isolated from the others so I could bring her home right away.

But I would have to be content with this temporary arrangement, and as Jim reminded me, at least it was only a short drive to go check on her and take her something to eat several times a day.

The next morning I called our vet, Dr. Brooks. His partner, Dr. Allen, was able to come out later that afternoon to draw the blood for a Coggins test to make sure the little mare didn't have anything contagious to other horses. I gave him directions to where the property was located from my house and told him that my truck would be parked right there on the road. I arrived about an hour before the appointment, just in case the mare had wandered off to the back of the property and I needed to search for her. I wanted her up and ready by the road and didn't want to be searching for her on the vet's time.

She had indeed wandered off, and I felt very uncomfortable walking back onto this man's property, especially after what Doreen had said about his temper. I looked over at Doreen's place to see if her truck was there. I was going to ask her if she would go with me to search for the horse since she knew Mr. Land, but the drive was empty. Oh, well, I decided, I can't just stand here. I threw the halter I had brought over my shoulder and started back through the weeds.

About halfway onto the property, I found her in a little clearing standing under a small oak, seeking shade from the blistering sun. Her back was to me and her head was hanging almost to the ground. My stomach sank at the sight of her. It was just as shocking as the first time I'd laid eyes on her the day before. "Hey, little girl," I called out softly. She lifted her head ever so slightly and turned to look at me. When I came closer she nickered a greeting softly back to me. Before I put the halter on to walk her up front, I hugged her head and rested my cheek against her forehead.

We were ready and waiting for the vet by the road. I was holding a bucket with a small amount of grain while the little mare ate, when a neighbor and friend of mine happened to drive by. Lori saw my truck parked out on the road and stopped to see what I was up to. She got out of her truck, crawled through the wire fence, and walked over to us, not saying a word, the look on her face and the anguish in her eyes speaking volumes. "My God, Mel," she finally said. "What's wrong with people!" Lori and I had a lot of the same philosophies and she believed as strongly as I did about making a commitment to the animals who come into our lives. She had also never seen the mare all the times she'd driven by. I told her all that had happened the previous day, including the good news that the man who owned the horse said we could take her.

Lori decided to wait with me for the vet to arrive and I was glad that she did. Her upbeat attitude lifted my spirits. She lovingly petted the little horse and smoothed her mane, telling her that she was going to a good home and all her troubles were over. I was grateful to Lori and kept smiling at her as she spoke so kindly to the little mare. And I just felt so blessed that things worked out the way they did. What if the horse had never managed to get out of her prison in the back of the property? She surely would have died soon. And what if she had never wandered past that high weed line the day I was driving by? I never would have seen her. Or if I had gone to the feed store even an hour later or earlier and she had wandered back to the tree where I found her on this day? I was just so thankful that this little mare would be coming home with us and never hurt again.

Dr. Allen arrived right on time and pulled in behind my truck. As he stood up by the road, before crawling through the wire to where Lori and I stood with the starving horse, it was clear he was just as shocked at her appearance as the rest of us. He hadn't even walked over to us yet but quickly voiced his concern about what damage this severe emaciation was doing to her internal organs and warned me to take it slowly. I promised him I would.

After I introduced him to Lori, he walked around the little horse, gently touching her and checking her over from head to toe. As Dr. Allen was filling out the form for the state concerning contagious diseases in horses, he came to the line that asked her age. He looked into her mouth to judge how old she may be. After a brief examination of her teeth, he released her chin and looked down at the ground, shaking his head. "She's well under twenty . . . I'd say about fifteen. The poor thing looks thirty years old. This is unbelievable!"

He picked up his pad and wrote a few more things for the state, his face revealing the disgust he felt for the person who had done this to this poor horse. Then he glanced over at me, smiling, and said, "Well, what are ya gonna name her, Mel?" His pen was tapping the blank line on the form he was filling out that said "Name of Horse."

I told him that I hadn't thought about it yet and looked questioningly over to Lori. "Well, you found her on Sugar Bend Road. And she couldn't be any sweeter," she said as she pondered the possibilities. "Why don't you call her Sugar?" I looked at Dr. Allen with a big smile on my face and said "Sugar it is!" He smiled, and nodding his approval he wrote down "Sugar" with a flourish of his pen.

Just then some other neighbors of ours, a couple who lived further down on Sugar Bend, came driving by and stopped to see what was going on. They sat in their truck, shaking their heads at the sight of Sugar, as Lori and I told them all about her and that she was coming home to Proud Spirit just as soon as the blood work was back. And then, behind them, the gray-bearded man in the black pickup truck pulled up and he joined in the conversation about Sugar and her poor condition.

Dr. Allen was ready to leave and said he would call as soon as he had the results back from the lab. "The faster we get her off this property and away from this guy the better," he called over his shoulder as he walked to his truck.

While waiting for the results of the blood work, I continued to check on Sugar three or four times a day, taking her grain and carrots. I wormed her for intestinal parasites and I also brought my grooming bucket along and brushed her coat and doctored her wounds. Her stomach was a mass of open sores from being stuck in that swampy prison and being eaten alive by flies and mosquitoes. I put fly ointment on her stomach and sprayed her coat with a repellent designed for horses.

Every time I went to see Sugar I was always a little nervous about Mr. Land showing up. I didn't know how I would react to him face to face, but for Sugar's sake I had to remain civil, at least until we had her home, safe and sound on our property. And even then, I had no wish to confront this man and risk some sort of ignorant or violent retaliation from him against me, my property, or my other horses.

As the days passed, Sugar was becoming more and more used to my company and the regular meals I was bringing. She was always waiting at the front of the property watching for my truck. The nutrition she was receiving was starting to have an effect. She was holding her head up higher and her energy level was improving dramatically. Whereas before she would just stand and let me come to her, she was now walking to meet me at the fence line. Her coat was even starting to look a bit better. Brushing her, tending to her wounds, and keeping the insects off her was really paying off.

I felt exhilarated about her coming home and becoming a part of our family. I had an essential bond with this horse and was already very attached to her. She happily ate her grain while I held the bucket for her and chattered to her about this and that. Then she would stand quietly as I brushed and groomed her coat. She would lean her head against my chest as I hugged her to me and rubbed her face and ears, holding her close. She really was the sweetest little girl. Sugar couldn't have been a better name.

By all appearances, Sugar was actually in much worse physical condition than Annie was when we first brought her home to Proud Spirit. The difference was that Sugar was improving daily, no health complications were sapping her strength, and she was able to put all her energy into getting well. It seemed as though she was going to survive the starvation she had suffered under her cruel owner.

About five days after the vet had been out to see Sugar, my phone rang. It was Doreen. "Melanie?" She sounded upset. "Mr. Land just called me. He said someone he works with told him that you, your vet, and other neighbors were bad-mouthing him.

He's pretty mad and he said that you can't have the horse now. He said if you step foot on his property again he'll make you sorry."

I went cold and my hands started shaking. "Aw, God, no! Let me have his phone number, Doreen. I'll talk to him. There were other people there! It was everybody that kept stopping to see what we were doing. I can't control what everyone was saying!" Doreen gave me his number and wished me luck. I dialed Mr. Land's house immediately.

I couldn't believe this was happening. Even though I vehemently agreed with what everyone was saying that day, and probably had even stronger feelings of disgust for Mr. Land, I had learned from experience to keep my mouth shut. But I never would have dreamed that the gray-bearded man in the pickup would run and tell Mr. Land what everyone was saying about the emaciated mare, for he was calling Land worse names than anyone. And he seemed genuinely pleased that something was being done to help the horse.

But clearly it had to have been him. He was the only one of us there that day who knew Land personally. The other people who had stopped that day were my friends, and they simply would not do anything against me, or the little mare, for that matter. None of us even knew Mr. Land. It had to have been the man with the beard. But what possible motivation could he have had for destroying this mare's chance for a decent life? I just could not believe this was happening.

When I dialed the number Doreen had given me, a voice that sounded like a teenage girl answered and I asked to speak to Mr. Land. She asked who was calling and I told her my name. She put the phone down, and I heard a screen door slam, dogs barking in the background, and an engine running. Then the screen door slammed again and the young lady came back to the phone to tell me that her dad wouldn't speak to me. I pleaded with the girl to tell her father that there had been a horrible misunderstanding. I had no control over what others were saying and only wanted what was best for the horse.

She seemed indifferent to the dispute between her father and me but asked me if I did end up taking the mare could she come over and see her because "we sure love her." It was everything I could do not to explode and holler, "Then why aren't you feeding her!"

But I held my tongue, and trying to stay focused on getting Sugar away from these people, I told her yes, she could come visit the horse. I couldn't imagine welcoming them onto my property, but I would worry about that later.

I continued along the lines of asking the girl if she would help me convince her father that I had nothing to do with what the neighbors were saying. She seemed very happy to chat with me, and I didn't hear anyone yelling at her to get off the phone, so I decided to play on the girl's so-called love for the little mare. I told her about the health risks of not feeding an animal that is reliant on us for its care. I warned her that the little mare was pretty sick and I just wanted her to get well. Land's daughter was reacting positively to my depiction of the entire saga and promised me she would speak to her dad.

After hanging up with his daughter, I called Doreen back and told her that Mr. Land wouldn't speak to me.

"I didn't think he would by the things he was calling you and how mad he was. I'm sick about this, right to my stomach," Doreen said.

"What do you think we should do now?" I asked her.

"Let me think about it. I'll talk to my husband tonight after he gets home and see if he thinks he might be able to reason with Mr. Land." Like Doreen, I felt sick as we hung up. I wondered what I should do.

The next morning I decided to call animal control to see what they might suggest. When I spoke to the deputy who handles our part of the county he told me that he had gotten six or seven calls about this horse already in the last week. Ever since Sugar had managed to get out of her little pen in the back and show herself, it seems the entire neighborhood was in an uproar and wanted something done. The deputy was going out there to investigate the next afternoon.

I asked the deputy if he would drop the investigation if Mr. Land released the horse into Proud Spirit custody. "If there's no horse, there's no investigation," he replied. I was afraid of getting law enforcement involved, mainly because of the red tape, all the paper work, and the time it would take to get something resolved. It would be weeks before the sheriff's office could even begin to think about obtaining legal custody of the little mare, and Sugar didn't have a lot of time. And now that I was banned from going onto the property, she again wasn't being fed.

Confident that Mr. Land would prefer to avoid the sheriff's office pressing charges for animal abuse, I decided to call his number again. There was no answer, but I left a message on his answering machine. I was very careful how I worded the message and spoke very respectfully, as if we were in this together. I told Mr. Land that I just wanted what was best for the horse and didn't want to cause trouble, and in fact, I wanted to help him avoid trouble by taking the horse for him.

I let him know that others in the neighborhood had called animal control to complain about the condition of the horse and that a deputy planned to come out the next day to investigate. With his permission I would come get the mare first thing in the morning because, as the deputy said, "no horse, no investigation." I said this would all be behind us if he would just allow the horse to come home with me. I left my number on his answering machine, and then paced by the phone all evening praying for it to ring.

With all my heart, I had to believe this was going to have a happy ending. Sugar's health was improving daily. She was thriving from the attention we were giving her and had become very attached to me, and I to her. I already envisioned this precious sweet girl as a part of our family.

Close to ten o'clock that night the phone rang. I put my hand on the receiver but squeezed my eyes shut and took a deep breath before I grabbed it, willing it to be Mr. Land. "Please, please, please," I said aloud as I let out my breath and brought the phone to my ear.

"Melanie?" a woman questioned when I picked up. Damn! I thought. "Yes?" I answered hopefully. Maybe it was his wife.

"My name is April. I live a few miles down the other way from that neglected mare on Sugar Bend. I'm one of the people who called animal control about her. I knew you were trying to get her. I'm friends with Doreen, and we were all praying he'd let you take her. But, um . . . I've got some bad news, and I thought you should know."

I didn't say anything but waited for her to go on. I was gripping the phone hard, vaguely aware that my hand hurt. Suddenly, April burst out crying and through her choked sobs I heard her say, "He shot her!"

All the air left my lungs as if I'd been kicked in the stomach. My hand holding the phone fell to my side. I dropped my head and closed my eyes, squeezing them shut as I shook my head in disbelief. With effort, I brought the phone back to my ear, tears silently rolling down my face. April was crying openly, saying how sorry she was that she had to tell me this. And I knew without a doubt she was hurting for the little mare we had all tried to save, and that she was indeed sorry.

But she would never know how sorry I was. That one sentence, those four words that I left on Mr. Land's answering machine kept running through my head and haunt me to this day: "No horse, no investigation." Oh, Sugar, I thought. My God, what did I do to you?

I managed to ask April how she knew what had happened. Less than an hour before, April had been on her way home from work. She works at a small store out on the highway that stays open till nine. As she was driving past Mr. Land's property she saw him pulling in with a trailer. She decided to turn into Doreen's driveway, even though she could tell Doreen wasn't home, and see what he was up to. She turned off her car, then quietly went and sat on Doreen's porch.

April couldn't see anything from where she sat in the dark, but she could hear him opening the rusty trailer door, then the *thump, thump* of hooves on wood, and finally the trailer door squeaking closed and the latch sliding into place. April watched as Mr. Land pulled back out of his own property with the trailer in tow and she saw him go directly to the huge ranch across the street, where he apparently worked part-time. In the back of the trailer, April could see the shadowy figure of the emaciated horse in the glow of the moonlight as Land pulled through the gate.

She watched as his headlights cut a path down the long dirt road and continued on toward a small wooded area on the vast ranch. Then she saw the truck stop at the edge of the trees, the headlights still burning. April sat in the silence, straining to see or hear something, anything, but from this distance there was only quiet and darkness, except for those headlights.

Suddenly, April heard the sickening report of a single gunshot echo through the still night air. In shocked disbelief, April watched the truck and trailer come back down the dirt road and out the ranch's gate. Land pulled back in through his own gate, unhooked the empty trailer at the front of the property, and then went on his way.

When April and I hung up I felt like I couldn't breathe. I grabbed a beer out of the fridge and slipped on some shoes. I needed to get out of the house. I needed to walk among my horses, hear them breathing, and touch their healthy coats. I needed to feel their velvet noses, inhale their incredible, soothing smell. I started walking down our long driveway out toward one of our pastures, my vision blurred with tears. I stopped to wipe them away and ran the sleeve of my T-shirt across my eyes.

But when I lifted my face, I was surrounded by fireflies! They appeared to come out of nowhere but were everywhere . . . hundreds of them. Thousands. We had lived in this house for about two years, and I had never seen fireflies in such abundance out there. I couldn't believe my eyes. I turned in a circle, in absolute awe. The sight of their mere numbers was spellbinding. It gave me chills, even in the hot humidity of the Florida night.

And then from the pitch black of the pasture, seven of our horses silently appeared at the fence line. I hadn't heard the telling approach of a single footfall or the airy swish of a single tail. But there they were, the outline of their glorious heads and strong necks illuminated in the greenish white glow of this storm of fireflies, the tiny lights dancing along their healthy coats, sparkling and twinkling in their eyes.

I was laughing through my tears, and I asked out loud if the horses could see what I was seeing. They stood in a row along the fence, uninterested in my excitement over the fireflies, all looking at me eagerly as the carrot dispenser they had come to expect me to be. I smiled at them and told them I didn't have anything.

I set down my untouched beer and reached out at the air with both my arms, still not believing what I saw. Twenty fireflies lighted on both my hands and along each arm. Their tiny thread-like legs tickled and I smiled at the sensation as I shook them off. Then I crawled through the fence to hug my boy Strut. Putting my arms around his powerful neck and burying my face in his mane, I breathed deeply of his smell and told him what had happened to Sugar. I started to cry again. It was all too much, and I knew the only thing that would ease this pain would be time.

I couldn't figure out how someone could be so evil to put a bullet in that precious mare's head purely out of spite. It would have been one thing if he were ending her suffering out of love and compassion—and if so, there are certainly more humane and peaceful ways to do it than a bullet to the head. But this—to wrest her away from life in the night like a coward, when others only wanted to care for the little horse and love her—this was simply incomprehensible. I couldn't believe, after all Sugar had endured in her young life, that she should come to such a violent end.

Eventually, I wouldn't blame myself, or anyone else, for what happened. But right then I needed to be angry—at myself and the whole world as well. And I needed to cry.

But with the beauty of nature embracing us in the magical, auspicious glow of fireflies, my anger quickly lost its foothold. The relevance of trying to make sense of Sugar's vicious death was suddenly gone. I was instead immersed in the beauty of her spirit. Her overwhelming presence was a vivid and compelling reminder of all the good in the world, and I could seek refuge in the memory of the short week I was blessed with the opportunity to love her. I bent my head to Strut's mane and my arm encircled his neck from underneath, hugging him tightly. I reached behind me and placed my hand on the flank of another horse. The other horses stood near, heads down and resting. They seemed to sense my sadness and remained close, calm, and protective.

Silently, I gave thanks that the light of these fireflies would guide Sugar's gentle soul to me as I stood in the darkened pasture. I could almost feel her forehead against my chest and see her liquid brown eyes blinking slowly as I held her in my arms, and I found peace. I asked the force in nature that stands above us all to hold her just for tonight, and then tomorrow morning take her out to the greenest pasture and let her run, tell her she could run now.

In the days that followed, several of us spoke to the deputy about what we knew. He did go out to investigate the reports of animal abuse the day after Sugar was killed, but, as we expected, he found no horse. When Mr. Land was contacted, he told the deputy that he had decided to take the horse up to his sister, who owned a place a few hours from there with a lot of acreage, and that the horse was just fine. The deputy was satisfied with this and dropped the investigation.

Now when I drive by that filthy lot where we found that precious little mare, I keep my eyes straight ahead. Instead of picturing her as we all last saw her, emaciated and weak, and instead of recalling the horrific way she died, I see her fat and shiny, up over her hooves in lush green grass with a whole herd of other horses who have crossed over welcoming her into the fold. At least in that place, finally, she knows love and kindness.

Since the night Sugar was murdered and I stood in the pasture grieving for her with my horses, I have never again seen the abundance of fireflies that we were surrounded by on that night. And this quote always comes to mind whenever I remember Sugar and the way she would trustingly rest her head against my chest: "To be loved by a horse should fill us with awe, for we do not deserve it." ♘

Easy, Tango, and Charlie

"NOW, HERE ARE HIS TWO BLANKETS." The tall, elegant woman bent down and reached into a Rubbermaid tote, pulling them out. "This one, the thinner one, is for when the temperature is in the high forties to low fifties. The thicker one is for when it's in the low forties. If it's going into the thirties I put the thinner one on first, then I add the thicker one just before I go to bed." I wanted to tell her that horses simply don't need blanketing in Florida. Didn't she know that they have one of the most efficient systems for staying warm in the entire animal kingdom? Mares in the wild give birth in the spring at high elevations and drop their newborn foals in the snow without incident, and we're throwing heavily quilted blankets on healthy twelve-hundred-pound horses when it dips into the forties! She could probably recite the most difficult dressage test pattern from memory, but she didn't know that in temperatures of thirty to sixty degrees, horses are most comfortable in their own coats.

She glanced over at me to make sure I was listening to her

instructions about cold weather care. Her silky red hair was coifed into a perfect French twist, without a hair out of place. I kept thinking, How can anyone pack all the stuff she's brought out here, get a horse loaded onto a trailer and hauled thirty miles, and not have a hair out of place? It was amazing. She was still talking when I shook the thought from my mind.

"Here's his fly mask. And these are his two halters. One is a breakaway for pasture turnout, the other is for when he'll be supervised. I was going to give you his show halter, but . . ." She looked around my barn and silently took note of the glaring lack of blue ribbons and trophies. "Well, anyway, I think I'll keep it as a reminder of his incredible career." I thought I saw her swallow hard but couldn't be sure, for she just continued giving me instructions.

"Here are his daily supplements." She lifted a small cardboard box from the floor of the aisle way and set it on a table. "This is all self-explanatory. Each one has its own little measurer, and you just give him one portion twice a day, at each feeding."

She turned her back to me and rotated each jar so the label was facing forward. I took advantage of that moment to look heavenward and roll my eyes. I removed the clip that was holding my hair and ran my fingers through it, trying to get it pulled back off my face. The loose strands were blowing in the wind, tickling my cheeks and adding to my mounting irritation. She pivoted on one foot and said, "Okay?" I marveled once again at how neat her hair remained and was going to ask her for her secret, but instead I said, "Okay."

She returned to the stack of boxes and Rubbermaid totes, and dragged the largest one across to where I stood. I peered over her shoulder as she pried the top off, curious about what this one could possibly contain. She set the lid aside and revealed a vast display of grooming supplies. Groaning inwardly, I moved backward till my legs hit one of the resin chairs I kept in the barn. I plopped into it.

"Most of this stuff is self-explanatory," she said again. "It's all common grooming aids. However, I imagine he'll be out in the sun much more than he ever was with me. If that's the case his mane and tail will start to fade. I've brought some hair dye so you can keep his color maintained." She held the bottle of Miss Clairol at my eye level so I could see it clearly. Then she reached into the tote and withdrew what looked like a very large piece of chalk. "This is chalk. I'm not sure if you're familiar with this, but it's for his star, to keep it white. And this . . . " she began, and reached into the tote again. "This is for his hooves. To keep them black," she said, holding up a can of polish.

That was enough! Hair dye? Chalk? Hoof polish? I'd reached my limit and could sit quietly no longer. The horses at Proud Spirit are groomed daily, but they are groomed for cleanliness so they retain a healthy coat and skin, not so they can step into a show ring. I took my glasses off and rubbed my hand over my eyes before I spoke.

"Um . . . Vicky," I said as I let out a deep sigh.

"Victoria," she corrected.

"Yes, sorry. Victoria, when you and I discussed Easy retiring here, we talked at length about what we expected from each other. I told you in no uncertain terms that I did not believe in over-grooming horses who are retired. I also asked you not to shave the hair in his ears or clip his whiskers before you brought him out, but you did. They need that hair! It's there for a purpose."

She looked away from me and stared into the tote full of enough herbal shampoos, enhanced conditioners, braiding combs, and hairbrushes to supply the dorm of a large all-girls boarding school.

"This is very hard for me . . . " she said, her voice trailing off.

"I understand that, but why are you so focused on his appearance? Why can't you find some peace in the fact that he gets to just be a horse for a change? He gets to actually be in a herd, like he was meant to be! He gets to swim in the pond, roll in the sand."

153

She winced visibly when I said this and shook her head faintly, trying to rid herself the image of her beloved show horse, who had never had a hair out of place, covered in a layer of sand.

"Listen," I continued, "you have given Easy everything you possibly can. He's had every luxury and advantage. You've taken him further in the show ring than most people ever dream about. And he's given back to you everything he has to give. But enough is enough, and his body is worn out. Now let me give him the retirement he deserves, the retirement he's earned. Let him be a horse. Please."

"I don't begrudge him a retirement. My difficulty comes from the reality that without my care he will very soon look like the rest of your horses." She quickly turned around to face me. "I'm sorry, but that's the way I feel. I despise seeing horses with whiskers and hair in their ears. Unkempt manes and shaggy coats. I hate it!"

I knew the day I met her that Victoria and I were two very different people. And that's okay—diversity is good. But our differences went far beyond the fact that she shows horses and I do not. It is true that I have absolutely no interest in showing and that I question the ethics of some aspects of retaining blue ribbons. But I certainly do not resent people who show. I have numerous close friends who do it successfully without buying into the attitude that denies a horse his or her spirit. I resent the forced confinement and isolation from other horses, or any discipline that allows—indeed encourages—surgical procedures, barbaric shoes, and harsh bits to attain the desired look. I resent the attitude Victoria so selfishly displayed now.

We looked into each other's eyes, Victoria and I. Both of us unsure about what to say after the revelation of disgust she felt for the way I took care of my horses. She broke eye contact first and walked to the end of the barn.

"I don't understand your *routine* here." She said the word sarcastically, as if no routine actually existed. "I've been out here twice and I've never seen any of the horses in the stalls. Why are they always out?" She waved her arm toward our pastures and the horses grazing there.

I had a fleeting urge to tell her maybe she should load Easy back onto her trailer and repack his grooming supplies and leave my property. But I held my tongue because I loved this horse.

Victoria was not aware of it, but I had known Easy many, many years earlier. Before she had ever laid eyes on him or set foot in a show ring with him, even before she had bought him eight years earlier, this horse taught me about the equine spirit and the amazing partnership that can exist between human and horse.

Back when I was still floundering around with Cody, dangerously trying to teach myself to ride a horse I had no business riding, I lamented my woes to a friend who told me that I needed to feel what it was like to ride a horse that had been raised with kindness and participated willingly. This would give me something solid to work towards. The horse was Easy. And I will never forget the gift he gave me.

All these years later, I heard that he had suffered a back injury, and while he was relatively pain free, he could no longer bear the weight of a rider. I also heard that his current owner was going to give him away. We had never met, but I immediately found a way to contact Victoria and earnestly offered Easy a home for life at Proud Spirit.

"Let's agree to disagree about this," I said to her back. "I don't know what you see when you look out there, but I see twenty-six extremely happy, healthy horses contentedly grazing in a lush pasture, secure in the comfort and companionship of the herd. It is a complete mystery to me why this peaceful scene torments you."

"There's something *you* don't understand. Easy is used to a different life. He's never been out in the rain. He's never had to fight for his position in a herd. He's not used to being covered in sweat and sand. I'm going to come back in a few weeks to check on him. If I feel that Easy has settled in, then I'll leave his papers with you at that time and he's yours. If not, I will come back to get him and find him a more suitable home." She stalked to her truck and the trailer that brought Easy back into my life, and was gone. I could only shake my head and feel very sorry for her.

For a brief moment I was concerned about the possibility of Victoria actually taking Easy back. I was thrilled that he was here with us and did not want to lose the opportunity to provide the gentle bay horse a peaceful retirement as a thank you for all he had given over the years, to me and others. But I let my concerns fade to the background, for in the days that followed Victoria's warning, I had more urgent matters to contend with. I was trying to organize transport from Tennessee for two abandoned Thoroughbred geldings. Both were less than two years old and were near death from starvation, or had been at the time they were discovered on the vacated farm.

A gentleman named James Darby had called me several weeks before to ask if we had room for the two babies at Proud Spirit. James is the loan officer of a bank in Knoxville. His branch had recently foreclosed on a small farm about twenty miles from town. After the bankruptcy was complete and the property vacated, James took a young couple who had hopes of purchasing the farm out to see it.

"We were walking around the pastures and the woman thought she heard a whinny come from the barn. Sure enough, there were two little colts in there. In the same stall! No food, no water. We had no idea the previous owners just abandoned them when they were evicted," James told me.

"Unbelievable!" I said. "How long were they there?"

"Almost two weeks, we think. You could see fresh teeth marks all over the stall where they had been eating the wood. It was pretty awful," James recalled.

The young couple subsequently bought the farm. They happily agreed to take care of the two horses till a home could be found. The bank reimbursed them for their time and paid to have both colts gelded. It was about a month after the two youngsters were discovered that James found us, after he had called around to a few different rescue organizations. None he contacted had room at the time. He was finally directed to us, and we agreed to take them. Now we just needed to find a way to get them to Florida.

I started making phone calls to different professional horse shippers. I wanted to find one that might have two empty stalls, was coming south, and would possibly transport the geldings for free—or at least for a reduced rate. I found a company out of Ocala, north of us, that was coming from Lexington, Kentucky, in about a week and a half with several empty stalls. They agreed to stop in Knoxville to collect the two little guys, and they even agreed to do it for free.

The day before I expected the horses I got a call from the driver of the van they were coming in. He called to tell me they had numerous other stops but would probably arrive at Proud Spirit sometime around five or six the following evening. I was excited that they were on the road and anxious to get them here. I asked the driver how they were.

"Well, they're pretty scared," he told me. "Real nervous and high strung. I decided to open up a partition in the van so they could stand together. That seems to have helped. We had a little trouble with them at the layover last night outside of Georgia. I turned them out in a small paddock so they could stretch their legs. When it was time to reload, we had a devil of a time catchin' 'em. Like I say, they're pretty scared. And they sure are attached to one another. Once we got 'em back in the van I spent some time petting them and trying to get them to calm down."

"Thanks for being kind to them. They've been through a lot," I said.

"Oh, that's no problem. Glad to help. And by the way, they *look* like they've been through a lot. I understand you haven't seen 'em, that right?" he asked.

"No, I haven't. In fact, I've never even spoken to the girl who was taking care of them. I knew they were pretty skinny when they were found about six weeks ago, but I have no idea how well they've recovered. And I was told they both have pretty bad legs—some deformities that will prevent them from ever being ridden," I stated.

"Yeah, their legs are bad. Not so they don't get around, mind you, but they'll never be usable. As far as their weight, I'd say they don't look too bad, just a little bit of rib showin'. The thing that makes 'em look so awful is that both are shedding their winter coats and it doesn't look like they've ever been brushed. There's these great big globs of hair hanging off 'em. And they're covered in this nasty claylike mud. I mean covered! Never seen anything like it! It's almost funny! Get your soap buckets ready!" He chuckled and I couldn't help but laugh too. I was so thankful the babies were being taken care of by this gentleman. I told him I was looking forward to meeting him.

"Well, we'll see ya tomorrow evening!" he said, and I hung up the phone feeling very good.

The following morning the phone rang at about eight o'clock. When I picked up, it was Victoria.

"I'd like to come check on Easy this morning. Do you mind?" she asked with no preamble.

"No, I don't mind at all. C'mon out," I told her while inwardly grumbling to myself about her lousy timing. I wanted to concentrate on preparing for the two new arrivals. Now I had to bring Easy in and give him a thorough going over. I would make sure no sand was clinging to his coat and that his mane and tail were tangle-free. He had settled in beautifully with us and I knew he was happy in the life we provided, but I had made a vow to myself that for Easy's sake I would placate Victoria and her vision of how she thought he should live. And so when she decided to come out to check on him, he would be spotless. If she approved, she would give us his papers and Easy would be ours forever.

When Victoria arrived, I had Easy up in a stall for her, munching on his grain. I had spent a good hour grooming him, making sure he looked clean and neat. She asked if she could bring him out to the aisle way and spend some time with him. I answered in the affirmative and then left them to go about my daily chores with the other horses.

I was down in one of the smaller back pastures tending to the four horses there when I noticed her walking toward me. She looked angry. I let her come the entire distance rather than meeting her halfway. Maybe with the extra walk she'd cool off about whatever had her upset. When she reached my side, she pointedly asked, "Don't you bother to doctor wounds?"

"Of course I do. What are you referring to?" I asked. I had just spent an hour going over Easy's entire body. I hadn't seen a single cut or scrape on him.

"Would you please come look at this and explain why it's being neglected?" She didn't wait for my response but turned and started back to the barn. I trudged after her, gritting my teeth and reminding myself that Easy was worth this, and much more.

"There," she said, pointing to a little scuff about the size of a half-dollar where the hair had been knocked off Easy's leg. But the skin was not abraded. "This is what I was talking about the day I brought him here. Why hasn't this been doctored? I don't understand this neglect."

Neglect! I was dumbfounded. Horses get this sort of thing every day. This was nothing! Victoria must have taken the stunned look on my face for guilt, for she foolishly continued, "You know, I was looking at that elderly horse by the gate, right there. To me, she just looks neglected. I don't want Easy to end up like that. I'm just not quite sure what my feelings are about all this."

"Well, I'll give you some help figuring it out," I said when I finally found my voice. "That mare is almost thirty years old and has a thyroid disease. She looked a hundred times worse the day she arrived. I'm very proud of the care she receives and how far we've brought her. And regarding Easy and that little tiny nothing you just pointed to on his leg, all I can say is, you have got to be kidding! You have been rude and insulting every time you've come out here and I've just let it go, but this is petty and ridiculous. How dare you question the care I give these horses and accuse me of neglect!"

"Well, I didn't mean to insult you," she stammered. "I've just never seen horses that look like this. So *natural*, I guess, if you prefer that word. You need to understand that this is an entirely different world to me."

"No, now *you* need to understand something. I will not defend myself to you anymore. Nor will I put up with your rude behavior on my own property. Look out over these pastures and decide if this is the life you want for Easy, free of charge. If it isn't, go home, Victoria, and get your trailer. Come back out here today, and I mean today, and take him back to wherever you were boarding him, and you can resume paying an absurd amount of money for him to stand in a stall all day and be bored out of his mind. Your decision."

She started to speak, but I looked over her shoulder and noticed a truck pulling a horse trailer turning into our driveway, so I interrupted, "I don't have time to discuss this any further. I've got two new horses arriving today and I need to go greet them." It was only about eleven in the morning. They were early, but I was thrilled. I left Victoria at the barn and rushed to wave them in.

"I'm Dave. We spoke on the phone," he said, extending his hand after he had parked the truck with the trailer carrying my two new boys. He was a pleasant-looking man with friendly blue eyes and a warm smile. I reached out to return his handshake as I said, laughing, "You're early!" Dave told me that he had decided to drive through the night and get to Ocala. The two geldings had been getting agitated and didn't appear to be tolerating the trip very well. He had unloaded the big shipping van and the other horses and had brought them in an open stock trailer the rest of the journey. "They're pretty upset," he added.

"Well then, let's get 'em outta there," I said as I nodded toward the trailer. I could see through the bars of the trailer that they were definitely nervous and scared. Both looked a little thin but not too bad. And Dave wasn't kidding when he said they were covered in dried mud with tufts of shedding hair hanging off them everywhere.

"Where do you want them?" he asked.

"Let's just open the trailer door and let them right into this paddock here. That way we won't even have to halter them and they can get calmed down on their own without us putting our two cents in," I said.

"Sounds good," Dave replied as he unlatched the door and let it swing wide. The horse at the rear of the trailer, a little sorrel with a white star, would be the first to come off. But for some reason he wouldn't step down. We backed away so he could take his time deciding how he wanted to do this. Suddenly, he started to buck, still in the trailer. He turned sideways and gave one final blast that hit the swinging divider, then he bolted from the trailer in a frenzy and ran to the far fence line.

The little guy appeared to be okay. I said to Dave, "Geez, what brought that burst of energy on?" He just shook his head as the remaining horse started to scream for his companion. Dave hopped up in the trailer to free the divider so the dark bay could join his pal.

I saw Dave tugging on the latch, but it didn't release. He looked up to the ceiling of the trailer with a perplexed expression on his face. He reached up with his right hand to wrench the top bar. "What's wrong?" I called over the noise of the horses. The horse in the trailer was turning in a frantic circle and screaming at the top of his lungs. His thrashing weight was making the trailer pitch and sway and clatter noisily. The freed horse was running in a pounding circle as well, 'round and 'round the trailer, screaming for his trapped friend.

"The divider is wedged into the frame of the trailer! It must have happened when he kicked it!" Dave exclaimed. "Do you have a sledge hammer?"

I ran up to the barn and into Jim's shop. As I flew past Victoria, who was still standing at the back of the barn, I noticed that she was looking wide-eyed and panicked as the bay horse violently fought to be free of the trailer. I found the sledge and raced back to Dave, who was standing by the stuck divider. The little gelding had started to buck and was ignoring Dave's attempts to calm him down with soothing intonations, "Settle down, boy. . . ." The distraught horse was soaked with sweat. It was springtime, but our temperatures were already hot and humid, and these guys were acclimated to the colder weather of their home state. I was worried that he would become overheated. With each passing second, the dark bay's terror and confusion over what was happening seemed to intensify. We had to get him out of there.

Dave saw the danger for both horses as they continued to scream and display their anger over this separation. He glanced at me over his shoulder and yelled above the noise, "This is probably gonna make him flip out, but I don't have any choice!"

"Do it!" I yelled back.

Dave lifted the sledge hammer and brought it down hard on the bar of the divider. The resounding clang reverberated through my ears, but the gate swung free. The tortured gelding was frantic as he dashed the few steps to the opening, to freedom. The two horses quickly found each other and planted themselves together.

I let out a ragged breath and shook my head, thankful that we had averted tragedy. I had thought the horse that had been trapped in the trailer would surely explode. Dave walked over to me and let the air out of his lungs as well. "Man, that could've turned ugly. I can't believe that happened!"

"Thank goodness no one got hurt, including you! I was worried that when he kicked, his hoof was going to come through the bars and knock you cold," I said.

We both turned our attention to the horses. They were standing as far away from us as the fencing would allow. Both were out of breath, their sides heaving as their laboring lungs struggled to replenish the oxygen. Rivulets of sweat dripped from their chests, bellies, and faces, making the matted hair and mud more pronounced. They looked absolutely bedraggled and pathetic.

In all the chaos I had forgotten about Victoria. I turned to her, still at the barn. She appeared frozen in place and looked as though she would crumble to the ground if the level of shock was ratcheted up one more notch. Both of her hands were clenched into fists covering her mouth, and she was crying—not openly, but silent tears were slipping down her cheeks.

I cursed under my breath. I was in no mood to offer her comfort, but started for the barn. "Are you okay?" I asked when I reached her side.

"My God! How do you do this? How do you handle all this? They're just babies! How can you bear the pain they're in? I couldn't bear it!" She groaned all this through her bunched-up hands.

"This is what neglect looks like, Victoria." I pointed to the two geldings who had slowly started to settle down and regain their breath. "Not the horses out in this pasture with unclipped manes and whiskers on their muzzle. And I can handle the pain these babies are in right now because I know I'm going to make a difference in the way they'll live for the rest of their lives."

Victoria left without another word. Later that day, I found Easy's papers sitting on a table in my tack room.

I named the two abandoned babies from Tennessee Tango and Charlie. They are going on four years old now and have grown into strapping, strong, and healthy teenagers. They have both gained the confidence and curiosity they should possess at this age and absolutely love our attention. And while they remain remarkably attached to one another, each has established his own position in the herd and cultivated new friendships with other horses. I couldn't be more proud of them.

Easy also found his place in the herd. With each passing day

163

he began to look and behave like a real horse. For many years, he had been asked to do the equivalent of sitting idle in a lounge chair all week and then participating in an athletic competition when the weekend arrived. We wouldn't be so foolish as to do that, yet we expect our horses to and are mystified when they're "off." But horses need to move. The pain and physical limitations resulting from Easy's years of being confined to a stall and a demanding show career diminished considerably once he was allowed the freedom to move about naturally on thirty acres.

He thrived emotionally as well. Once in the security of the herd he immediately found companionship with another gelding. They became best buddies and Easy would initiate hours of mutual grooming and physical interaction—something he had been denied for so long, but that is deeply essential to a horse's well-being.

When I think about all that Easy has given, I feel a peaceful contentment in knowing that we can give something back to him. ⋃

Charlie, on left, and Tango, enjoying their newfound freedom at Proud Spirit.

Rodeo

I WAS FIFTEEN YEARS OLD WHEN MY SISTER, Manitta, eighteen years my senior, gave birth to her sixth child. Sarah came into this world screaming and didn't stop until she was two years old. This beautiful little baby had endless stomach problems that redefined the word colic. My exhausted sister spent what seemed like every waking moment holding and rocking Sarah, rubbing her stomach, rubbing her back, trying to comfort and ease the painful cramps and spasms. The doctor's office became their second home. But miraculously, as soon as Sarah turned two, the colic ceased as if a switch had been flipped. And practically the first sentence out of her mouth was, "I want a horsy!"

I don't know of anyone in my very large family ever owning a horse or even having a passion to ride, so where Sarah got this seemingly inherent equine love is a mystery to us all. Even our maternal grandparents, who had a small farm in Michigan back in the forties and fifties, didn't keep a horse. But Sarah must have been born loving horses, and as she grew she needed to be around them like she needed air to breathe.

Although she wouldn't have her own horse until she was an adult, Sarah spent her Florida summers as a young teenager learning to ride on a giant Draft–Quarter Horse cross named Buck. I don't recall now how they met, but Buck belonged to an older gentleman who lived out in the country and who allowed Sarah to ride the horse whenever she pleased. This beautiful dun gelding was as gentle as he was huge.

I remember going along with my sister to take Sarah out to ride Buck. When other kids her age were spending time at the beach, Sarah preferred to go see Buck. She would hop onto Buck's back—no saddle, no halter—and she would lie on her stomach facing his tail, with her arms across his enormous hind end and her chin resting on her hands. Buck would slowly walk around his pasture, contentedly grazing with this kid who was madly in love with him draped across his back. Buck is gone now, but he still holds a special place in Sarah's heart.

After high school, Sarah went off to college in California, where she earned a degree in Animal Science from San Louis Obispo's equine program. Then, thank goodness, she came home to Florida. We were thrilled that she was relocating near us, and her help and input with the sanctuary have been invaluable. There have been times when I don't know what I would have done without her. Sarah found a job as the manager of a local feed store that caters to a large equestrian population. She also hires out to train horses around the area, and one of the most impressive aspects of her success with horses is that she believes in working with the horse's owner as well as the horse. I agree with her wholeheartedly and couldn't be prouder of her accomplishments. Surrounded all day by horses, horse people, and horse products, Sarah is in heaven.

One afternoon while I was still at work I got a call from Sarah. Her voice was full of barely restrained excitement. "There's a surprise waiting for you when you get home from work!"

"What is it?" I asked with a laugh at the anticipation in her voice, knowing full well she wouldn't tell me.

"I'm not telling," she said. "Just don't leave the gate to the paddock open till you look around good."

"Well, then it's not a surprise. It must be a horse if it's in the paddock. C'mon, what's the story?" I prompted.

"It's not a horse, but he really needed a home and I left you a note on the kitchen counter explaining everything. Call me when you get home! Bye!" I called her a little rat for her impish prank and for not telling me what I was coming home to, but she had already hung up.

She said it wasn't a horse. I kept asking myself what it could possibly be. Could it be a llama? I didn't know a thing about taking care of llamas. Or maybe it was a donkey. That would be okay, I thought. Then little Cleveland would have a same-species buddy. As dear and priceless as Cleveland had become to us, I would take in a hundred donkeys if they were only half as sweet as he was. A goat, perhaps? Oh, Sarah, I thought to myself, it better not be a goat! A goat would fit right through that gap in the paddock gate and be into Lord knows what by the time I made it home. We simply aren't set up to take in a goat—surely Sarah knows this. . . .

I have a pretty good view of the paddock coming up our long driveway. Craning my neck, I could see nothing as I approached the house. When I pulled up to the carport adjacent to the barn with an even better view of the paddock, I still could see nothing. Oh boy, I thought, whatever it is, it must have escaped.

I turned off the truck and hopped out to survey our property, but from where I stood nothing looked amiss as it would if a liberated goat had been wreaking havoc on the farm. Unless—oh, no!—unless the little devil had found the feed room! I ran for all I was worth up to the barn but stopped short at the threshold to the room where we store our grain. The door was secure. I scratched my head and leaned back against the door, crossing my arms over my chest, pondering what, and more immediately, *where,* this little surprise of Sarah's might be.

Completely stumped, I pushed off from the doorjamb and was about to walk back to my truck when I heard the ever-so-slight, airy swish of a tail. I turned my head toward the aisle of the barn where the noise had come from.

"Oh, my. . . . Well, hello there!" I said to my "little surprise," a smile involuntarily coming to my lips. When Sarah said it wasn't a horse, she must have been trying to throw me off. Granted, he was only about thirty-four inches tall, but he was indeed a horse. He stood absolutely stock-still, smack dab in the center of the aisle, warily eyeing me from underneath a thick and unruly fore-lock that almost reached the center of his nose.

The sun was glowing behind him, and motes of dust were drifting in the beams of pale yellow light, making him look ethe-real and otherworldly. He was a rich sorrel color with a pure white face and he had the wildest, thickest, craziest flaxen mane I had ever seen. It stuck up all around the top of his head in these great spikes that made him appear as though he wore some fabu-lous and elaborate African ceremonial headdress fit only for a high chief. You simply couldn't help but smile when you looked at him; he was absolutely darling.

I started to walk towards him, talking softly, but he startled me with a neat flick of his flaxen tail, and in an instant the little horse was gone. He ran out the back of the barn, his head cocked to the side as he made his escape. It looked as though he was try-ing to keep one terrified eye on me, and then he came skidding to a stop in the farthest corner of the paddock. He wheeled around to face me, eyes wide with fear and glaring at me as if I had burned him with a torch.

Not too fond of humans, I thought to myself, and wondered what his story was. I remembered that Sarah had said she would leave me a note. I went in the house to find it. "Mel, this is Red. Isn't he adorable!" she wrote. "He has been horribly abused and you won't be able to get near him. He really needs to be here with you and receive the love you can give. Hopefully he'll learn to trust again. Call me and I'll fill you in on the nightmare he has lived. He's only four years old." He was indeed adorable, no doubt about that. But the whimsical feeling I'd experienced just by looking at him turned to a deep sadness that he should be so desperately afraid of humans.

I walked back outside after reading Sarah's note, making a mental note to call her later in the evening. Red had not moved from the far corner of the paddock. His gaze was still fixed on the barn, and he seemed convinced that I would emerge at any moment and cause him harm. I decided that now was as good a time as any to begin showing the little horse that he would not be harmed. I had grabbed a bag of carrots from the fridge, but they weren't for Red. I wanted him to get a feel for his new home before I even attempted to go near him, and I wanted him to see that horses were treated kindly here.

I walked out to the fence line, in the opposite direction of where Red stood, and behaved as if I didn't even know he was there. Red never took his eyes off me, pivoting his body to keep me in his direct line of sight. I casually walked over to JJ, who just happened to be standing at the gate of the large pasture.

JJ is a great big, gentle, twenty-three-year-old Quarter Horse gelding. He had come to us about a year before. He is not rideable because he has arthritis in all four legs. JJ gets along just fine, even with his limitations, but Proud Spirit is his retirement and here there will be no more toting anyone around. He had belonged to an elderly couple who loved him dearly and took beautiful care of him. But when the wife died, the husband didn't feel he could tend to JJ anymore and approached us about taking the horse to live out his life at Proud Spirit.

I started breaking off chunks of carrot for JJ, making a big elaborate display of loving on him while he chewed what was in his mouth. Dramatically I stroked his neck, saying, loud enough for Red to hear, "Good boy, JJ, good boy." Then I'd give JJ another chunk of carrot and do it all over again. I kept my back to Red but angled just enough so I could watch him out of the corner of my eye.

We were about on the fourth or fifth carrot when I saw Red's tense body, ready for flight, begin to relax. I still didn't look in his direction but instead kept plying JJ full of carrots and petting him with mushy theatrics. Red slowly, tentatively, dropped his head and started to graze, still keeping his eyes fixed on JJ and me. Finally, he relaxed even a tiny bit more and turned his head away from me. *Perfect!* That was all I wanted.

I thanked JJ for being so cooperative and apologized that the carrot feast he had just enjoyed was over. And then, keeping my back to Red as if I still didn't even know he was there, I casually walked back into the house. The vague idea that I wasn't a threat had been planted and that was enough for the day.

That evening I called Sarah at home to get the whole story on Red and how he had been brought into our lives.

A customer of Sarah's at the feed store had come in one morning to ask Sarah if she knew of anyone who would take in a severely abused Miniature horse. Sarah told the woman all about Jim and me and our sanctuary. She seemed to think the life we could provide for the little horse would be exactly what he needed. Sarah asked her customer for more details about the abuse and where the horse was located.

"He's at my house now," she told Sarah. This woman apparently had a neighbor who was trying to raise Miniature horses and train them on his own to pull carts. He appeared to be quite wealthy; his home and property were very nice and everything was in excellent repair. He had about seven mini horses and several expensive-looking carts. The horses were all very well fed and beautifully cared for, physically at least: feet trimmed on time, top-of-the-line feed, clean stalls with fresh shavings. But the man didn't know a thing about communicating with horses, and in his ignorance he tried to train these little guys using fear, pain, and intimidation.

Sarah's customer had witnessed horrible abuse that included the man screaming at the horses and whipping them till they fell to the ground trembling in fear. He used pliers on their tender little mouths and ears as a form of restraint. He had no clue whatsoever about how to train the horses to pull a cart. He would tie one of their back legs up off the ground to the rigging of the cart. Once the cart was hitched he would drive the horses with their one leg still tied! "To keep them from running off," he said. All of this trauma on the horses was compounded by the man's heavy drinking and explosive temper. But there was one horse who took more abuse than any of the others. This was the man's stallion, Red.

There are good horse people who know how to handle mares and geldings but don't know a thing about how to handle a stallion. It takes a special understanding of what motivates these horses to safely keep them. When you combine a total ignorance of horses with the naturally strong-willed disposition of a stallion, you have a disaster waiting to happen. This was certainly the case with Red's situation. The only way this ignorant man knew to communicate with Red was to soundly beat him.

Sarah's customer had tried to talk to the man several times, keeping it friendly and non-confrontational, but he just laughed off her softness for the little horses. Having gotten nowhere, she called animal control. Unfortunately, unless the abuse was witnessed by law enforcement or the horses were starving and there was no food on the property, there was nothing they could do. This was not the case, for all the horses' physical needs were being met. So the mistreatment continued for months.

One day the abusive man walked over to Sarah's customer's house and told her he had had it with trying to do anything with the "stupid creatures." He was selling them all, including the carts and rigging, and wanted to know if she was interested in buying anything. She felt as though her prayers had been answered and was thrilled he was getting out of horses, but she could not buy anything he had for sale. In the next few weeks she saw a few people coming and going, carts being loaded onto trailers, as well as some of the horses.

Several more weeks went by before the abusive man, once again, came walking up her driveway, obviously intoxicated. But this time he had one of the horses with him. The miniature horse was trotting behind the man as he yanked him along with a lead rope, and any time the little horse faltered the man would turn and slash him across the shoulder with a whip. It was the little stallion, Red.

The woman saw this happening from her barn and came running out to stop him. When she met him halfway up her drive she didn't even have time to speak before he said, "I can't get rid of this one! He's scared of his own shadow and no one wants him. He's yours." He handed her the lead rope and an envelope containing the horse's papers and then he turned to walk away. The little horse stood trembling, frozen in fear, his eyes wide with terror—with good reason, it seems, for he knew what was coming. As the drunken man walked past the little horse, he raised his whip in the air and brought it down as hard as he could, slashing Red loudly across the hind end.

What was even more telling of the abuse these horses must have endured while in this man's possession was the fact that when the little horse was hit with the whip, he never moved a muscle except to brace himself for the pain. He must have learned that if he reacted by moving even one inch, the beating would continue.

Sarah's customer didn't really want the little horse, but she certainly wasn't going to insist that the man take him back. She decided she would just let Red settle down for a few weeks and she'd worry about finding him a good home later.

This kind woman paid to have Red gelded and devoted as much time as she could to helping him learn to trust again. She was making some headway and he was calming down somewhat, but she didn't feel she was doing enough. Red was still terrified of people and had to be kept in a stall, as he was impossible to catch if he was turned loose. Once he had a halter on and someone held his lead rope, he stood like a little soldier. He would tremble with fear, but he showed not one ounce of fight. That had obviously been beaten out of him. Sarah's customer wanted what was best for the little horse and felt he needed more than she could give. It was then that she happened to speak with Sarah and that Red came to be part of the family at Proud Spirit.

That morning following Red's arrival, I walked out to the paddock where we were keeping him. The second he caught a glimpse of me he bolted to the farthest spot he could find. He turned to face me down, his nostrils flaring and his eyes wild with fear. Every muscle in his entire body was strung taut like a bow. I'd never seen anything like it.

I decided to give him more time before we started getting serious about being introduced. After all, he had just arrived the day before. He was in strange surroundings and, without a doubt, he was going to need a lot of time to adjust. I didn't even want to put him through the fear of coming near the barn while we were around. So to feed him, I simply put his grain in a rubber pan on the ground out near the spot he felt the safest and let him eat after we had walked away. I fed him this way for several days and just tried to leave him alone.

I decided to continue with the carrot feast ritual I had started with JJ the day Red arrived. I wanted Red to see that horses were not screamed at or whipped at his new home. And so every day, with whichever horse was lucky enough to be hanging out by the gate at the time, I would try to show Red that horses were treated kindly. I would bring one of them into the paddock and stand far enough away so as not to be a threat to Red, but close enough so he could see and hear what was going on. And I always kept my back to Red while I doled out lots of carrots, lots of mushy cooing, and lots of gentle strokes down the chosen horse's neck. Red would watch this every day with mild but increasing curiosity.

Every day we could stand a little closer to him, and every day it took a little less time for him to relax enough to ignore us and start grazing while always keeping a wary eye on us. Then I would return whichever horse I had back to his own pasture and walk away from Red's space, never obviously looking in his direction.

One day, about a week or so after Red had arrived, I had JJ in the paddock getting the whole "treatment" again. (The smart boy was learning about the payoffs of hanging out at the gate.) I could see Red watching us with more interest than usual. It truly was interest, but it was clearly still mixed with fear. He started to inch closer toward us. I don't know if it was a need for human contact on his part or the smell of the carrots that was finally getting to him, but I was thrilled that he was approaching. I kept my back to him and relaxed my whole body. Then I put my head down and started to just rub JJ's chest instead of reaching up to his neck. I wanted my body language toned down if Red was going to try to come closer.

Among horses, the horse that causes the others to move out of his way is the one in charge. An almost imperceptible dominant look, a slight pinning of the ears, an unwavering stride, an instinctual understanding of body language between them—all these factors establish the dominant horse in a herd. I thought it would be good for Red's self-confidence if he saw JJ and me retreat from his advance in order to emphasize to him that he had some control in his new life, that his decision to approach, which he had made of his own free will, had a positive effect. We would give him his space, and space was what he so desperately seemed to need. Still not turning my body around, I asked JJ to slowly back up. JJ moved back about twenty feet. He had so much carrot in his mouth that bits of it were spilling out onto the ground with each grind of his teeth. I was hoping that Red would find the pieces and think that was a pretty nice treat.

After what seemed like an eternity I could finally hear Red behind me crunching on the bits of carrot that had fallen to the ground. I was so excited and so desperately wanted some interaction with him. This was such a huge step for him, to actually approach us! Whether he was spurred on solely by the carrots or not, I was thrilled. Slowly, slowly I turned around, quietly saying, "Good boy." But the instant I spoke Red was gone in a blur and had run to the far corner of the paddock. Dammit! I blew it! I could have kicked myself for my impatience.

Red's sudden bolt startled JJ. He stopped chewing his mouthful of carrot as he and I both watched the little horse darting away. JJ slowly shifted his gaze from Red's position of safety directly to me, still not chewing his carrots. I could feel his reproving stare scolding me for opening my big mouth. I sheepishly looked back at JJ and said aloud, *"Sorry!"* And only then did JJ resume chewing. I could almost see him shaking his head at my stupidity as I returned him to his own pasture.

In the days that followed we knew it was time to start working on Red accepting our touch. He had been allowed these previous days to settle in and get to know his new home. But it was time for him to start becoming more at ease with his new caregivers and learn that he would never be harmed again. We began every day by setting his feed pan a little closer to the barn, then walking away, letting him eat in peace. Once he was fairly comfortable by the barn—which he was as long as we stayed away—we started to set his feed pan at the door of a stall. This process went on for an additional week.

Eventually, we started to set his pan of grain inside the stall door. He still would not let us near him. He had been with us a little more than two weeks and we still had not even touched him.

There may have been quicker ways to get little Red up to the barn, but it would have been a fight and in my opinion it would have been emotionally violent. It would have destroyed any small fragments of trust we had managed to build up to this point. We may have had him where we wanted him physically, but he would have been lost to us forever, emotionally and spiritually. And that simply wasn't worth it to me; nothing would have been worth that trauma just to make things easier on ourselves.

When the day arrived that Red did walk into a stall to eat the grain we had placed there, I quietly but quickly came from behind and closed the door on him, with mixed emotions. Sarah was there with me that day. We decided that in the confines of the stall we would try to lure him to us with a soft voice and some treats. We let him eat his grain in peace and then gave him some time to digest his food. Now it was time to get introduced.

Sarah went into Red's stall first, clutching a handful of carrots. We knew this wasn't going to be easy, but neither of us was prepared for little Red's reaction and what would happen next. Sarah had intended to kneel down and show Red the carrots she was holding, but the instant she walked in and closed the door, he turned in blind terror and literally ran himself into a wall, hitting it hard. I was watching from the aisle way, looking over the half door of the stall. My stomach lurched in agony for this poor little horse, and I squeezed my eyes shut at the sound of his body slamming into the wall. When I opened my eyes, Sarah had turned to face me, our eyes locked, the deep sadness on her face mirroring my own. Both of us felt sick to our stomachs about what little Red must have endured and what it had done to him.

"We're just going to have to do it, Mel," Sarah said. "He's got to see that we aren't going to hurt him. The sooner he knows that, the sooner he can start to heal."

I nodded in agreement and entered the stall as well. Together, Sarah and I slowly worked Red into a corner of the stall. His eyes were rimmed in white and wild with fear as he pushed his nose into the corner. He kept turning his head frantically side to side, trying to keep both Sarah and me in his line of sight at the same time.

We both put our outside arm against the wall so he wouldn't turn to bolt. Then Sarah reached forward with her other hand and gently touched Red's hind end. His reaction to Sarah's touch was very, very disturbing. Little Red started to tremble so violently we thought he was going to fall down. He almost went to his knees, painfully reminding both Sarah and me what she had been told about Red and his mates being beaten till they fell. It was awful to watch, and Sarah and I both had tears in our eyes.

Sarah was talking softly to Red while she continued to gently touch his back. But Red was not accepting any of it. His muscles strained and twitched against Sarah's hand. The violent shaking in his legs was so severe it was causing his head to bob. We had been standing near him for no more than one minute and had been touching him for less than that, but when his profound fear of us overtook him so that he lost control and urinated down his legs, we understood we needed to back off and let him be. We got completely out of his space and allowed him time to calm down.

Sarah and I stood in the aisle of the barn. Neither one of us spoke as we tried to absorb what had just happened. His vehement terror of us, of humans, was so troubling. We were as perplexed as we were horrified as we tried to imagine what this horse had gone through to make him react in such a way. I remember Sarah staring down at the concrete floor of the barn, almost imperceptibly shaking her head. She leaned back against a stall and slid down the wall, resting her elbows on her knees, her chin in her hands. I turned my back from where Sarah kneeled and walked to the end of the barn, shoving my hands into the pockets of my jeans. I looked out over our pastures and saw our other horses contentedly grazing. I wondered if we would be able to help little Red heal. I wondered if he had been pushed too far.

After more than a week of cornering Red in his stall and attempting to gently touch him, we really hadn't made any progress with him at all, so I decided we needed to switch tactics. At the time that Red came to us, we had been dealing with abused horses for almost eight years. I had seen some pretty awful cases, but nothing like this. We had dealt with timid and shy horses, horses who were nervous and scared, and even some who were pretty fed up with humans and had become violent and hard to control. We were proud that every single horse who came here had found peace, security, and a dignified life, as well as a strong bond and trust for the people who loved and cared for him or her. But Red's fear of humans was beyond anything we had ever seen and we needed a new game plan. We needed a very powerful tool to help us communicate with Red. That tool, I decided, would be his own mind.

Red had been with us just about a month or so. He knew all the horses on our property as each had been introduced to him two or three at a time in his paddock. There had not been one moment of squabbling between any of the full-size horses and Red, and we decided it would be safe to turn Red out with the herd of fifteen horses in the large thirty-acre pasture out front.

The plan now was simply not to expect anything from Red. Nothing. We were going to set him free with the herd and pretty much just ignore him. We would feed him, of course, and check to make sure he was healthy and uninjured, but it would be from a distance. Red could come and go as he pleased; he could move in the security of the herd, come as close to us as he dared, and that was it. We would force nothing on him, especially ourselves. When he was ready to come to us we would be here, ready and waiting. Until then, he could learn and discover, completely on his own, when or if he wanted anything to do with us.

Our horses are kept on lush pastures year-round. The growing season slows way down in the winter here in our part of Florida, but we are blessed with enough healthy grass to sustain us through the winter. All the horses are brought in every single day and fed their portion of grain in a stall. Each is groomed and checked over, and then all are turned back out—unless, of course, one of them is injured or ill and needs to remain inside where he can be properly cared for.

Once we decided to set Red free, I simply opened the gate to the big pasture, then stepped back to let Sarah herd Red through. It wasn't hard. All she had to do was walk behind him and he bolted to get away from her. Circling the paddock that had been his home up till then, he quickly found the open gate. Slipping through, he never looked back. With his mane and tail aloft, and all four feet pounding, he galloped out to his waiting new herd.

I knew this was a bit of a risk. If for any reason we needed to tend to Red, we would never be able to catch him roaming free on thirty acres. But all my instincts were telling me that his emotional health was worth the risk. If we pushed ourselves on him at all, he would be destroyed and we had to take this chance to prevent that. It was all up to him now.

In the days and weeks that followed, we tried to pretend that we didn't even know Red was there. We avoided making eye contact with him, and we never walked in his direction or directly towards him. When I called the herd in from the front pasture to the paddock each day to be rotated into the barn for mealtime, Red came in with them, naturally, but stayed as far away from us as he could manage. We continued to feed him in a little rubber pan out where he was most comfortable, setting it on the ground and walking away before he would come near to eat. But we always had to feed him last, after the rest of the herd was turned back out or secured in a stall, so they wouldn't run Red off and eat his portion of grain. Some days, you could tell that he was getting impatient with this routine, having to wait till the others were fed. But he never made it clear that he was ready for us to treat him differently and we continued to "ignore" him.

Several months passed, and in the daily comings and goings of taking care of the horses, it was clear that Red's attitude toward humans had not changed one bit. If we came anywhere near him to reach another horse, he bolted. And to turn him back out with the herd, we just had to open a gate, step back, and let him fly through.

One afternoon, my friend and neighbor Carla was over. I

was talking to her about the ongoing struggle Red was having with his trust of humans and how it seemed like we were making no headway. Suddenly Carla interrupted me and said, "Red! You're still calling him Red? All these horses that you like to give a symbolic fresh start with a name change and you haven't changed *his* yet? Geez, Mel! Of all the horses that need a fresh start . . . ," she said quietly as her voice trailed off and she turned to look at Red.

"Yeah, you're right," I said as I followed her gaze and watched him over by the fence line, eating his grain. "But nothing's come to me. I give them a new name as I bond with them, or get a feel for their personality. I've barely even touched Red, let alone bonded with him."

Carla and I talked for a while longer. When she was ready to leave and walk across our pasture to her own home, I decided to go ahead and let Red out, as he had finished eating. We were heading toward the gate, in Red's direction. Seeing us approach, his head snapped up from picking at the fallen bits of grain. He quickly went on the alert and bolted about twenty feet from Carla and me, then turned to face us, ready to bolt again and get farther away if necessary. Carla laughed at him and said, "You silly fella! Nobody's going to hurt you here!"

She shook her head, still laughing at him, finding his insistence at holding onto his fear of humans somewhat comical. "Look at him," she said. "He looks like a little rodeo clown out there dodging bulls. The way he runs and then turns to face us— always staring down the danger, but keeping his distance, just like a rodeo clown. Even his pure white face looks like the clown's. Silly fella."

"That's it!" I shouted with my hands in the air. "Rodeo!"

"What?" Carla laughed.

"Rodeo! That's what we'll name him!" I said. "It's perfect! It even reflects the new attitude we should have. We need to quit letting out these great sighs of sadness every time we look at him. Whenever he runs from us, it breaks our hearts and all we do is think about his past and the hurt he has suffered. We're the ones who aren't letting it go! Instead, we need to smile at him and laugh at his silliness and, as you say, his rodeo-clown antics. And we need to think about his future. A happy future!" I felt uplifted and said his new name again, "Rodeo! It's perfect!" Carla agreed with me.

Over the next several days, it was an effort to adopt this new attitude towards our little Rodeo. It still broke my heart each time his profound fear of us showed itself and caused him to keep his distance. But I truly felt it was in everyone's best interest, especially Rodeo's, if we behaved less sullen towards him, both inwardly and outwardly. It was time to stop walking on eggshells around him and act a little more natural.

During this time there were instances when we had to put Rodeo's halter on and tend to some of his needs—like grooming him, letting our farrier trim his feet, or worming him. This was always pretty traumatic, but we had no choice. The only way to accomplish this was to corner him in a stall, work up his side, and slip the halter over his head. Once the halter was in place, he lost all his fight. He was still terrified and still shook, but he didn't show a bit of fight. We took these opportunities to try and calm his fears, kneeling down to his level and slowly and gently touching him all over. We would let him back away just the length of the lead rope when it would become too hard for him to bear our touch, but we'd ask him to come close again once he had a chance to settle down. We eventually worked these sessions into a daily routine. His progress, though slow, was astounding. I was so proud of the trust he was beginning to show. But he still trembled and shook when we were near, although not as much, and he still had never actually come to us.

One particular morning, I was having a bad day. Aside from

everything going wrong that could go wrong, I had an appointment in town—an appointment that required me to be clean and showered. It's not so bad when you can do your chores around the ranch, then hop in the truck "as is," so to speak, and go do your errands. But when you have to start your chores, stop what you're doing, get cleaned up and change your clothes, then go into town, and then come home, change back into your work clothes, and finish your chores, it makes for a lot of extra work, and I wasn't in the mood. I fed the horses that were in the two back pastures, but the others out front would have to wait till I returned home. I was clean and ready to leave for my appointment when I noticed Taffy in from the front pasture, standing at the gate to the paddock.

Taffy is a little Palomino mare who came to us a few years ago. She is as sweet as can be and had been a therapeutic riding horse at an academy for disabled children for many years. Taffy developed serious back problems and could no longer be ridden, even by small children. We brought her to Proud Spirit so she could retire. Taffy loves Rodeo with all her heart and behaves like he is her foal. And for all of Rodeo's independence in the herd— for he couldn't generally care less what the rest of the horses are doing—he is frequently close by Taffy's side.

While most of our horses love the freedom of their pastures and the company of the herd, Taffy loves to be up near the barn. I saw her that morning, standing at the gate looking a little sad, and I decided to let her into the paddock. I quickly ran out to where she stood, trying not to get the as-of-yet-not-picked-up piles of manure on the soles of my good shoes, and opened the gate for her to come in. From out of nowhere, Rodeo came blazing down the fence line and slipped in beside Taffy before I could close the gate. Oh, well, I thought. They can just hang out in here together till I return home. I started back through the barn to leave when Taffy called out with a hungry whinny. There was plenty of lush grass for her and Rodeo in the paddock, but she wanted her grain.

"Oh, Taffy!" I said as I kept walking. "I'm in a hurry, girl.

You can wait, can't you?"

She called to me again; it was just enough of a plaintive cry to get to me. I turned around with a sigh and looked out back. Rodeo was off, happily grazing, and I decided to go ahead and give Taffy her lunch. Muttering to myself about these darn horses, I grabbed a bucket from the feed room, threw in a scoop of grain, and walked back out to Taffy, holding it for her while she ate. I couldn't simply set the bucket down and let her eat; if I walked away, Rodeo would come over and join in. This would be too much grain for him and he'd be blown up like a tick. So I was stuck till Taffy finished. Granted, this was all of my own doing, but I was stuck nonetheless.

It's funny how things happen in life. I was so preoccupied with my appointment and the fact that I had once again been a sappy pushover for a whinnying horse, I didn't even realize what was happening. I was chattering away to Taffy, telling her not to dawdle over her lunch, while I kept looking at my watch. All of a sudden I felt a little velvet nose in the crook of my elbow. It was Rodeo trying to pull the bucket that I was holding for Taffy down to his level so he could get at the grain.

"Knock it off, Rodeo. You'll have to wait till I get home," I said with some irritation. Then it hit me like a ton of bricks! Rodeo was touching me! He had come to me and was actually touching me! One wrong move from me and he would be gone. I had to let him know that his brave step would yield results, positive results. I was grinning from ear to ear, but without turning around, I lowered the bucket to Rodeo's level in response to his pulling at my arm so he could eat a few bites of the grain. Taffy had no problem sharing her portion with little Rodeo and just lowered her head along with the bucket.

I felt a little breathless . . . so excited . . . but I kept up my chattering as if nothing was out of the ordinary. I had to behave as if it was normal, everyday stuff for Rodeo to come to me and let me know he would like his lunch also. When he had eaten what I felt was enough grain for his little stomach, I gently nudged him away and positioned myself between him and the bucket while Taffy continued eating. Rodeo wasn't happy about this and we spent the next few minutes in friendly competition, him trying to get at the grain and me trying to keep him out of it. At one moment, I made an effort to honor my vow to not walk on eggshells around him anymore. An unforgettable thing happened. I turned sideways and tipped my head down, looking him right in the eye. He stood less than a foot from me, his little face at just about the level of my belt. He was looking right back up at me. For the very first time since coming to Proud Spirit, Rodeo's eyes were not drowning in fear. They were not rimmed in white, wild with the terror he felt of humans, nor were they darting from side to side, searching for an escape. He had come to understand, on his own, that I would not harm him.

We stood like this, staring into each other's eyes. I slowly started to smile. Tears of elation were making my eyes glisten, and I whispered to him, "You're going to be all right, aren't you, pal?"

In the following weeks and months, Rodeo continued to commune with us, and his trust still grows dramatically, each intangible milestone enriching all of our lives—but especially his own. Rodeo eventually came to a place in his recovery where we could place our hands on him without his legs trembling at all. He is learning the benefits of a soothing and kind touch. I can now stand over him and hug his little body to mine without his muscles straining to keep some distance, and he is discovering the pleasures of being gently groomed or having one of us scratch his back. I can now kneel down, my face close to his, and kiss his forehead and softly rub his eyes closed without him recoiling in fear. He actually allows himself to relax and become sleepy with the comfort of a gentle massage.

We are ever mindful of the journey Rodeo has taken and how far he has traveled to be with us to be a part of this family. There are still some memories he is unable to release. If we raise an arm suddenly, as you would to wave away an irritating fly or to secure a hat that is about to be blown off by the wind, Rodeo still braces himself for the abusive slash of the whip that he felt so often during his young life before he came to us. And there are times when he still runs from us, unsure of our intentions or perhaps unable to endure a close proximity to humans. We respect his needs but continue to encourage him to participate, of his own accord, in his new life and his new family.

And every day as we watch little Rodeo confidently running free in the herd or galloping across the pasture for the pure joy of it, we are so thankful for the chain of events and profoundly aware of the blessings that brought this little horse to our home. ♘

Little Rodeo boldly crossing the creek at Proud Spirit to come in for lunch.

Marshal and the Outlaw, Wrangler

♘

SOME PEOPLE COME IN AND OUT OF OUR LIVES for different reasons. I have always believed the same in regards to our horses. We may not always be aware of it, but some have come to us because we needed them, and others have come to Proud Spirit because they needed us. Marshal definitely needed us.

For fifteen years the giant Belgian draft horse had worked as an integral part of a team pulling a heavy Western hitch wagon in competition races all across the United States. His superb, calm, and extraordinary power had turned him into a champion lead horse who more often than not landed his owner in the winners' circle. But whether or not Lee Williams deserved all that recognition, along with those trophies and blue ribbons, is another matter altogether.

It could not be disputed that he was a skilled driver, for he consistently put that wagon into so sharp a turn while whipping the team to maintain a pounding run you were sure the entire rig was going over. But it never did, not in front of an audience, anyway. No, the evidence was there at every sanctioned competition and fair that Lee Williams performed: he was quite a horseman. What was questionable about Lee Williams, about every aspect of his highly competitive personality, was, in fact, the manner in which he got his horses to do what they did.

Outsiders were not allowed at his training facility. And the only people he hired were wide-eyed and very strong young men who knew nothing about horses or their spirit. He preferred the people he hired to be ignorant. Lee would teach them everything they needed to know. The sole job requirement was that they look at Lee and everything he told them with reverent awe, as if he were a god, and only then would he give them the heady title of "trainer." In a very short time, these young men would become cocky and self-assured as they learned from Lee how to get a two-thousand pound animal to do their bidding. And very soon they would be swaggering around the fairgrounds of whatever city they were performing in, telling pretty girls they were one of Lee Williams' top horse trainers.

Although Lee didn't like it, he was occasionally forced to allow outsiders to come to his facility—farriers, feed store delivery people, and vets. And once in a while he needed to hire a photographer to take pictures of him and the horses—rigged up to the wagons in all their regalia—for the brochures he had made up about his performances. The organizations that enlisted him to demonstrate his skills paid good money.

Sage Douglas was excited when she got the opportunity to photograph Lee at his training facility out in the country. She had never heard of him before, but she loved horses and could certainly use the money. Though her work was outstanding, it was tough for Sage to make a living as a freelance photographer. As for Lee, he did not hesitate a moment when Sage quoted her fees.

When the session was over, Sage felt pleased with the way things had gone. The giant draft horses had behaved exemplarily and had stood hitched to the wagons with the discipline of soldiers. Lee Williams had been efficient and cordial, if somewhat aloof. He seemed to prefer one of the trainers to relay his instructions and wishes for the photographs he wanted taken. In fact, when they were finished, he simply gave her a cursory nod and left the grounds.

Sage watched him walk away. She could still hear the sound of his spurs clinking after he was out of sight. Curious, Sage couldn't resist inquiring from one of the young men who were busy unrigging the horses.

"What's with that ax handle hanging from his belt?" she asked. She had noticed it tethered to a loop in his jeans by a short length of latigo.

He turned to face her and smiled. "Didn't you notice the size of these guys' heads?" he answered casually as he patted the big gelding on the neck. "How else do you think we train 'em to keep their heads down?"

"You're kidding, right?" Sage responded. She did not get an answer but was sure he was just teasing her.

When she returned a week later with the proofs of the photography session, she would learn that what the young trainer had said was no joke. Sage unintentionally arrived at her appointment with Lee a little more than an hour early. This would turn out to be serendipitous for the powerful lead horse, Marshal, but horrifying for her.

As she walked toward the aisle of the barn, she heard a man screaming. No one noticed her approach over the yelling, and when she rounded the corner Sage stood immobilized with shock.

The Palomino gelding had somehow gotten tangled in the leather straps of his breast collar. Sage saw him step sideways directly onto the reins, and Lee was screaming at him to back up, hitting him across the chest with the ax handle. Suddenly the massive horse drew himself up to his full height and tried to move back, snapping the leather. When the expensive reins broke in two, Lee went into a rage.

"You stinkin' bastard!" he screamed through gritted teeth as he swung the ax handle at Marshal's head. "Back up! Back up! Back up!"

Marshal responded to the blows to his head the way he had been trained. He obediently brought his head down, inadvertently hitting Lee in the face. The two stable hands instinctively backed up when they saw Lee's rage turn to a fury bordering on the insane. An animal-like roar escaped his throat as Lee spun around and blindly grabbed a two-by-four he kept leaning in the corner. In one swift movement, he swung it like a bat directly across Marshal's eyes. The gentle gelding squeezed his eyes shut and dropped his head further toward the floor as Lee brought the weapon back down across his face. This time Marshal was brought to his knees, and the giant horse, who was only trying to comply with what had literally been beaten into him for fifteen years, crumbled to the hard concrete, unconscious and still.

There was no doubt in any of our minds: Marshal needed Proud Spirit. He never recovered from being hit across the face and began to suffer seizures from neurological damage as a result of the violent trauma he endured. He became "useless" to Lee Williams. In the brief time that she dealt with the training facility, Sage Douglas learned that Marshal was going to be euthanized and quickly intervened on his behalf. She contacted us to see if we had room for him. We immediately said yes.

Very soon after his arrival he settled into his new life with a contentedness that seemed to accumulate daily. Jim was quickly, deeply taken with the sweet horse. We all were, really. We couldn't get over how gentle he was. He would lean his huge head against Jim's chest and rest there for as long as Jim continued to stroke his face and softly rub his eyes.

We were sickened to the depths of our souls the first time we witnessed Marshal suffer a seizure. To see this graceful, gentle horse helplessly thrashing on the ground as a result of someone's violent temper was gut-wrenching—especially after it was over and the big horse clamored to his feet in a state of sleepy confusion, actively seeking us out for comfort, begging for us to hold his head and tell him it was okay. I can honestly say it was the first time in my life that I wished another human being would burn in hell.

In the months that followed, we would manage the seizures and ensure that Marshal had the dignified life he deserved. He was clearly adapting to this new home we provided and he simply loved to be near Jim. However, we were troubled that once turned out in the pasture, he seemed to prefer to be alone. He had not bonded with any other horse. We would observe Marshal on the fringe of the herd, always keeping his distance from the others. There was no doubt that he was content, but he just didn't seem happy.

One day I was scooping grain into my big bucket on wheels to finish feeding the second shift of our twenty-eight horses. The phone in the tack room jingled and I ignored it, like always, subconsciously counting the four rings that would then signal the answering machine to pick up. I rarely let the phone interrupt my routine during the day, choosing instead to return calls once I was finished with my work and in for the night. But whoever it was must have hung up when the machine answered, for no message sounded. The phone rang again. I decided to grab it.

"H'llo," I said.

"Oh, good, I got ya. I'm lookin' for a gal named Melanie."

"I'm Melanie. What can I do for you?" I said.

"Well, somebody told me you like horses. I'm hopin' you can take this little wild one I got runnin' around my yard," he said with a laugh.

I did an automatic head count anytime someone said this to me. Jim and I handled the care of our horses and the financial burden without help. We were in a bit of overload. Yet somehow we always seemed to manage just fine anytime we took in "just one more," and after that "one more" was firmly established into our family, we couldn't imagine the horse *not* being here.

There was a comical edge to the voice of the man on the phone. I couldn't help but smile as I asked him what the story was.

"Sort of a long one. Ya got a minute to talk?" he asked. I turned and took note of the fifteen horses standing at the gate waiting for their turn to come in for lunch.

"Sure," I said. I was still intrigued with his tone of voice and already liked this guy.

"Well, I'm single," he flatly stated, as if this somehow cleared up the mystery of why he needed to find a home for "the little wild one" running around his yard. I remained quiet and waited for him to continue.

"And, well, I don't have no pets. Not even a dog," he said.

"Mmm hmm," I mumbled, curious about where this was going.

"And see, some of the boys I work with keep on pesterin' me about needin' a pet. It's somehow become this big joke. Truthful, I fail to see the humor. But, well, you know how some guys can be."

"Mmm hmm," I responded again, smiling to myself.

"Well, my birthday come around a few months ago. Me 'n a coupl'a the boys went out to shoot some pool, have a few beers— that sort a thing. Then I went home. But they all insisted on followin' me back to my place. Hell, I thought they just wanted to have a few more beers! But when I pulled in my gate I'll be danged if there wasn't the smallest dang horse I ever saw standin' there in my carport with a dang bow around its neck! I at first thought it was a dog!"

"No kiddin'," I said.

"No kiddin'! Why, the little rascal only come up to my knees. Never seen anything like it!" he laughed.

"Huh. . . ." I responded, still smiling at his story.

"So, anyway, the boys all thought that was real funny, buyin' me this three-month-old colt as a pet. They stood out there slappin' each other's backs, laughin' their fool heads off. Then the jokers left. And I'm left sittin' here with this poor little feller that looks like he just wants ta know where his mama is."

"He's just three months old?" I asked.

"Well, he's eight months now. I sorta falled for the little rascal and let him hang around. But now I realize he needs to be with other horses. I grew up with horses and this little feller's not learnin' any proper behavior, if ya know what I mean. And truthful, he's startin' to get pretty full of himself."

"I imagine he is. It's bad enough to be weaned at three months! His mama didn't get a chance to teach him anything. But to be completely alone without another horse when he should be learning some horsy social skills! That's even worse! He's probably a little devil!" I exclaimed.

"Well, you got that right. He's startin' to rear up at me and buck. Just today he bit my leg, and dang if it didn't hurt! I just don't have the heart to scold the little feller. But I figure I better do something. It's not fair to him," he said.

The following weekend, Randy Miller loaded the little pet Miniature horse into the back of his work van and hauled him out to Proud Spirit.

"Oh, my gosh!" I cried when I saw him. "He is adorable! What's his name?"

"I call him Wrangler," Randy answered.

"It suits him," I said with a nod.

Wrangler's back came to just a little past my knees. His fuzzy dun-colored coat was baby-fine, and he had a pronounced, dark brown dorsal stripe running down the center of his back. I was immediately smitten and bent down to hug him.

"Watch it!" Randy warned, just as Wrangler pinned his tiny inch-and-a-half-long ears and tried to bite my face. I avoided his bared teeth and immediately formed my fingers into my own set of teeth and "bit" him back on the side of the face, just as his dam would have done had he tried that with her. The little horse was startled and looked at me with renewed interest. Not once in his short little life had he been reprimanded.

The next thing that captured Wrangler's attention was all the horses. We turned him loose in the paddock and he was absolutely beside himself. He ran along the fence line, bucking and yelling and tossing his head. It was a pure delight to watch this little baby who had not seen another horse in five months bursting at the seams in his joy. He kept running up to Randy and me, then he would spin around in front of us as if to say, "Do you see all these horses!" as he sped back off to the fence line and the horses there. We laughed and laughed at him.

After a few minutes of this, Wrangler finally settled down a little and came back to stand beside Randy and me. I was rubbing his forehead and scratching his mane, but he just couldn't seem to resist showing me what a big man he was. With a very sassy look on his face, he bowed his neck up and took a few short high steps, and then plastered his rump against my legs and started bucking!

"Well, you little rat!" I exclaimed as I shoved his back end around to make him face me. Even though they were so small, those sharp little hooves would certainly hurt me if they had connected with my leg. I made him back up by waving my hands at his chest, trying to establish some dominance. Wrangler gleefully reeled away and tore off around the paddock once again, bucking and whinnying at the top of his lungs. His behavior was hilarious. I had never seen such an inherently happy horse! Randy had been watching Wrangler's attempts to assault me with a sheepish grin on his face.

"I told ya he's a little full of himself," he shrugged.

"We'll work it out. He just needs to learn some manners," I said with a laugh.

One of my elderly mares was standing at the gate to the paddock. I decided to let her in with Wrangler and let them get introduced. Pie came to us a few years ago because of a shoulder injury. She is extremely maternal and very gentle. It is typical for her to instantly adopt any newcomers and make them welcome. Pie would be the perfect companion for Wrangler and would hopefully teach him some badly needed social skills.

The soft look in her eyes told me that Pie was immediately enthralled with Wrangler. She calmly trotted over to him with "open arms." She ever so gently leaned down to say hello . . . and he immediately tried to bite her! The little horse haughtily pinned those tiny ears and bared teeth that were no bigger than buttons on a shirt and actually tried to bite this full-size horse who could flatten him like a pancake if she were so inclined! Randy and I instantly looked at each other with matching shocked expressions on our faces. Wrangler's behavior was *preposterous*.

"Huh," we chorused to each other and then quickly returned our attention to the horses.

Pie began backing up, showing submission. Wrangler could sense her fear and readily used it to his full advantage. He confidently arched his neck and, with knees dancing high, he stepped forward till he was against Pie's legs, just as he had done to me a few moments before. Cautious yet not suspecting what was about to happen, Pie innocently looked down at Wrangler. Just then he started bucking. Shocked, Pie quickly turned in retreat and trotted away, attempting to put some distance between herself and this pint-sized tormentor.

Seeing the challenge, Wrangler happily tore after her and deftly maneuvered himself directly in front of Pie, who now came to a skidding stop. A look of horror mingled with disbelief crept across her face as the little devil reared up to his full height, such as it was, and tried to strike at her shoulder! Pie blew a burst of nervous air through flared nostrils and scrambled to turn in the opposite direction. She then ran to where I stood, seeking safety by my side.

It was obvious this pairing wasn't going to work. I made a lame attempt to calm her fluttering nerves and then returned poor Pie to the sanctity of her pasture. With a final accusing glance in my direction, she dashed off to her herd mates. I stood holding her empty halter in my hands and pondered this dilemma we now faced.

I needed to put a horse with Wrangler that was more aggressive than Pie but not so aggressive that he or she might hurt him. I pulled Cody out of the herd and put her in with Wrangler. Cody has always been very kind to other horses, and at the same time she's never been pushed around by any of the others. I thought this would be perfect.

She too gave Wrangler the benefit of the doubt and calmly walked forward to introduce herself, blowing softly through her nostrils as she approached. Wrangler's cockiness seemed to be inflated to a degree I don't believe I have ever seen before or since. It must have been the take-down he had just accomplished with Pie. He tossed his head in pure confident bravado and came at Cody with his front hooves flashing.

"Show him he can't do that, Cody!" I said aloud.

"Can you believe this little guy!" Randy laughed incredulously, shaking his head in disbelief.

Cody swung around in a blur and both of her powerful back legs blasted at Wrangler's flank like pistons. I wanted her to correct him, but not like that. He immediately dropped down and turned to run. But this strategic withdrawal of his was completely without fear; he acted like it was a game. One of Cody's hooves had caught him on the rump, and he had faltered but stayed on his feet. Unfortunately, Cody wasn't finished and appeared determined to completely eliminate the troublesome little horse. She ran after Wrangler with her head snaking back and forth like a rattler, and there was murder in her eyes. He was oblivious to the danger he was in, yet somehow managed to stay just a step ahead of Cody. This situation would never do. I grabbed a halter and took chase.

Once Cody was returned to her pasture, we decided to give this a little more thought. But Randy had seen enough, and with the promise to stay in touch, he turned to go. In our very brief meeting, Randy and I became fast friends. He is genuine and kind, and we have remained good friends since.

"Are you sure ya wanna take this little feller on?" he asked before he left.

"No," I laughed. "But I refuse to allow a peevish little colt who's too big for his britches to take command of this entire ranch!"

Randy shook his head and chuckled, "Well, you're a bigger man than me. I don't think I can watch no more of this!"

"*Coward!*" I teasingly yelled after him as he walked to his van.

The following morning I went outside to check on Wrangler. I was anxious to see how he had managed his first night at Proud Spirit. He was still confined to the paddock alone, but he could see the other horses and I hoped he found some comfort in that. The moment he glimpsed me he sprinted to my side.

"Well, are you gonna behave yourself today, you little monkey!" I queried.

He responded by sinking his teeth into my thigh. "Ouch! You little rat!" I hollered as I lifted my foot and popped him on the belly, again, just as his dam would have done had he tried to bite her. He quickly faced me, shocked once again that I would reprimand him, and he slightly backed away. I came at him with a firm posture to make him back up even more. He responded to my body language and moved away. "Now, that's enough outta you!" I scolded, rubbing my sore leg.

Just then I looked up and saw Marshal standing at the gate. "Hmmm . . . ," I said to myself as I looked from Marshal and then back to Wrangler. "Maybe, just maybe."

I walked to the gate but hesitated, my hand hovering on the latch. In the equine hierarchy, size means nothing; we had just witnessed that as little Wrangler traumatized Pie. So maybe Marshal's personality was exactly what Wrangler needed; he was tolerant and gentle but not easily intimidated. Still, this could prove to be a bit risky, even if they got along beautifully. One wrong move from Marshal, however unintentional, and Wrangler could be seriously hurt. After all, Wrangler's feet were about the size of a half dollar—while Marshal's were the size of a dinner plate.

But something seemed incredibly right about opening that gate and letting Marshal come through to meet this little outlaw who had just joined our family. I flipped the latch and swung the gate wide open. Marshal started through the portal in his lumbering, sluggish gait but stopped when he noticed Wrangler at the far end of the paddock. Wrangler noticed him at the same time. The little horse playfully tossed his head and whinnied out a "hello"—or else he was exulting in his happiness that I had just allowed fresh meat into the paddock for him to torment. Either way, he eagerly trotted to Marshal's side.

Wrangler approached with his usual flair, prancing and arching his neck. Marshal stepped forward to greet him. This is good, I thought, at least he's not backing away. The big horse turned his head slightly to the side, as though he were trying to focus in better on this little whirlwind that had just advanced into his space. Before Marshal had a chance to even think about it, Wrangler reared up and landed with both front hooves firmly planted on Marshal's broad chest. I squinted my eyes in a reflex to the panic that seized me and held my breath. All Marshal had to do was lift his tree trunk of a leg less than a foot off the ground and he could snap Wrangler's tiny leg like a twig.

Blessedly, Marshal didn't move while the little horse stood playfully on his chest. He turned his head squarely in my direction. He had acquired an extremely blasé look on his face that seemed to be saying, "This is some kind of joke, right?"

The little horse did not move either. And then, ever so gently, without lifting his feet, Marshal shifted his weight forward so Wrangler lost his balance and had to drop down. Wrangler turned in a jubilant circle, tossing his head and nickering in his delight! Then he reared up and did it again. This time Marshal leaned down to sniff the pest standing on his chest and was rewarded with a sharp nip to the chin. Completely unfazed, Marshal placed the side of his massive head against Wrangler's shoulder and eased him to the side and down from his chest once again. I was astounded! He could have easily flung him across the pasture instead.

Marshal moved off to graze and Wrangler went with him. But the little horse was not interested in the grass—no, he seemed to regard Marshal as his very own personal jungle gym and began weaving in and out of the huge horse's legs. He ran in circles and stopped only to quickly try and bite Marshal on his flank and then speed away. Through it all, Marshal remained passive and tolerant, but he gently corrected Wrangler when he took things a bit too far. And Marshal seemed to be acutely aware of Wrangler's whereabouts at all times, never lifting his feet too far or too fast. It was remarkable.

After nearly an hour, Wrangler finally played himself out and was ready for a nap. Contrite from having been repeatedly admonished, he sidled up to Marshal. Seeking shade from the sun, he stood directly under Marshal's stomach and snuggled against his leg to sleep. Marshal allowed himself this time to rest as well, and, not moving an inch, he softly shut his eyes. Shaking my head with wonder, I left them dozing like that and went about my chores.

A little while later I came back and found Wrangler awake from his nap, with renewed energy for romping. He had once again enlisted Marshal. But instead of just letting the little horse cavort around his legs, Marshal had actually decided to follow suit and frolic along! Since his arrival at Proud Spirit almost a year before, Marshal had barely even interacted with another horse, let alone played. But now he was tossing his head and gently trotting behind Wrangler in feigned chase. His eyes appeared brighter and more alert than we had ever seen them. He was actually animated. He seemed *happy!* It was a transformation I never imagined we would see.

The unparallel paths of two very different horses had merged to alter both their lives. Our little outlaw, by virtue of being himself, had somehow enabled Marshal to reconnect to his own innocence and all that it encompassed. The twenty-year-old abused and beaten Belgian had suddenly recalled what youthful happiness was. And little Wrangler was quickly learning the complexities of instinctual versus acceptable equine behavior, which would allow him the camaraderie he would need throughout his life.

Perhaps this proves that opposites really do attract. Maybe this proves the existence of fate, or the concept of yin and yang. Or maybe, just maybe, this proves that certain incongruities in life can result in miracles taking place right in our own backyard. ♘

The odd couple, Marshal and Wrangler, graze along peacefully, secure in their special friendship.

If you enjoyed reading this book, here are some other Pineapple Press titles you might enjoy as well. To request our complete catalog or to place an order, write to Pineapple Press, P.O. Box 3889, Sarasota, Florida 34230, or call 1-800-PINEAPL (746-3275). Or visit our website at www.pineapplepress.com.

Florida Horse Owner's Field Guide Second Edition by Marty Marth. Written by a nationally known equestrian journalist, this accurate, easy-to-read guide will help you select and care for a horse in Florida. Covers everything from purchase considerations to Florida's major conformation and color breeds to dealing with common hot-weather diseases. Includes updated state park, riding trail, and national riding club information as well as details on Florida's many shows and events for equestrians. ISBN 1-56164-154-5 (pb)

Myakka by P. J. Benshoff. Discover the story of the land of Myakka. This book takes you into shady hammocks, down the wild and scenic river, and across prairies, piney woods, and wetlands—all located in Myakka River State Park in southwest Florida. Walk, bike, or ride your horse through this remarkable ecosystem. With beautiful photos and line drawings. ISBN 1-56164-254-1 (pb)

The Exploring Wild series: A series of field guides, each with information on all the parks, preserves, and natural areas in its region, including wildlife to look for and best time of year to visit.

> *Exploring Wild North Florida* by Gil Nelson. ISBN 1-56164-091-3 (pb)
> *Exploring Wild Northwest Florida* by Gil Nelson. ISBN 1-56164-086-7 (pb)
> *Exploring Wild South Florida* Third Edition by Susan D. Jewell. ISBN 1-56164-262-2 (pb)

A Florida Cattle Ranch by Alto Adams Jr. and Lee Gramling. This is not just the story of one family's cattle ranch; it's also the story of one family's stewardship to the land and animals of Florida. Full-color photos throughout punctuate descriptions of wildlife, terrain, and cattle. A beautiful coffee-table book. ISBN 1-56164-159-6 (hb); ISBN 1-56164-166-9 (pb)

Poisonous Plants and Animals of Florida and the Caribbean by David W. Nellis. An illustrated guide to the characteristics of more than 300 species of poisonous plants and toxic animals, as well as symptoms of and treatments for their toxins. ISBN 1-56164-111-1 (hb); 1-56164-113-8 (pb)

Florida's Birds: A Handbook and Reference by Herbert W. Kale II and David S. Maehr. Illustrated by Karl Karalus. This guide to identification, enjoyment, and protection of Florida's varied and beautiful population of birds identifies and discusses more than 325 species, with information on distinguishing marks, habitat, season, and distribution. Full-color illustrations throughout. ISBN 0-910923-67-1 (hb); 0-910923-68-X (pb)